A Guidebook for a Pastor Search Committee

by

W. Glenn Doak

Desert Ministries Press
Matthews, North Carolina

A Guidebook for a
Pastor Search Committee

First Edition 2009
Copyright 2009

by

Desert Ministries, Inc.
P.O. Box 747
Matthews, NC 28106

ISBN # 0-914733-35-4

ISBN UPC 978-0-914733-35-5

In Memoriam

To My parents

W. Glenn Doak

and

Blanche Miles Doak

Who encouraged my Call to Ministry

and who both served on

Pastoral Nominating Committees

An Introductory Word
from Desert Ministries, Inc.

We at DMI feel that the subject of this book - choosing a new pastor – heads the list of the important things Congregations need to do. In some denominations to be sure, the matter is settled by the Bishop or the Diocese or other authorities, but among the Reformed and Congregational Churches that choice is a paramount decision. Normally the leadership of an organization largely determines the success or failure of the organization. Time to time I envy that hierarchical type of system where someone beyond the local church makes the decision: like in the Roman Catholic and Methodist traditions. It seems more objective and more in tune with the modern world. Yet I admit I gulp when I read that sentence. I was born, reared and still believe that it is the divine right of the local church to select its own pastor.

While the church does not belong to the Pastors who serve it, and while trained and meaningful lay participation is essential, still, if a bad apple can spoil the barrel, a wrong leader can surely spoil the congregation. In most churches, removing a pastor is a long and arduous struggle, unless there are obvious moral or legal infractions involved. But it still consumes the energy of God's people which should be directed to the future.

So, making the right decision in the first place, led by the Spirit of God and aided by a well trained Selection Committee is the primary duty of a Congregation which has lost its pastor. Dr. Doak has laid out some helpful detail on how best to help that happen. He also focuses attention on what the pastors you approach are thinking. I encourage you to read this book, even if you are not on a pastoral selection committee. It will alert you to the duties and responsibilities which every officer and member has for the future of their Church.

And one final word to the Pastoral Nominating Committee: Be careful. You might think that because you have been selected to help find a new minister that you are a heavenly head-hunter looking to hire a new employee. Dr. Doak makes it clear that is not the case. The best way to think about your task is that you are part of a process which is trying to identify the pastor God already has in mind for your Congregation.

As you and your fellow members go about your search, be careful, I repeat. You might think you are looking for a pastor, but actually the pastor is looking at you. The Committee is the only way the potential new minister has to determine if your church seems right for him or her. The search team is on view as much as the Pastor.

If you are interested in some other things that Desert Ministries does, we have added a list at the end of the book. We will gladly send a sample packet on request.

The peace of Christ be with you. Pray for your success all along the way. God bless you as you do.

Richard M. Cromie, President
Desert Ministries, Inc.
Charlotte, North Carolina

AUTHOR'S PREFACE

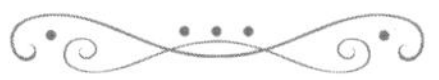

The writing of this book has been a long process of personal experience, gathering stories, listening to those who have served on Pastor Search Committees, then writing and rewriting the detail how a committee goes about its work under the direction of the Holy Spirit. Along the way many people have helped. There were the Search Committees in both Norman, OK, chaired by Jack Patten and Athens, GA chaired by Del Dunn who called me to Pastor their Congregations. I am grateful for that. Later, in both of those churches we learned a lot together as we sought God's will in calling Associate Pastors. Several Search Committees field-tested earlier drafts and made helpful suggestions including Southminster Presbyterian Church, Pittsburgh, PA; Westminster Presbyterian Church, Oklahoma City; and of course First Presbyterian Church, Athens, GA.

I would also like to thank the good people of Desert Ministries for encouraging me in the preparation of this book; especially John Mehl for his helpful editing work and Elly Fleming of the Publications Committee. I would also like to thank those who read a first or second or third draft of this book and made constructive comments along the way, Ray Dykes, Bob Forsythe, and Ed White.

I would also like to thank my dear wife Ginny for the hours she spent listening to me talk about the content of this book and the encouragement she gave me to finish it.

W. Glenn Doak, Athens, GA, January, 2009

TABLE OF CONTENTS

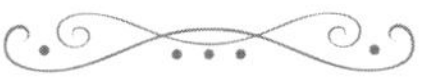

INTRODUCTION

This book is written mainly for members of a congregation who are searching for a new Pastor, or an Associate Pastor, and would like some help in deciding what a Pastor Search Committee should do and how best to proceed. It will address some key questions and attempt to answer them. The first major step is for the congregation to nominate and elect a representative committee to make the selection. There are various procedures in different denominations, but you are looking for those who will rely on their own experience, but are teachable and are open to the Will and Guidance of the Lord. Different denominations have different procedures to follow. An immediate contact should be made with the proper officials in your Church hierarchy to secure and apply the necessary rules and regulations. Otherwise you will stumble around and find road-blocks later in the process which can be avoided with a proper request for help.

This book will go on to discuss how the committee operates. Why is it necessary to be secretive about your work? What you are getting into if you agree to serve on such a Pastoral Search Committee. It will also suggest ways that individuals can become involved in the spiritual journey of discerning how God is preparing the congregation for the next chapter in its life. Most churches follow the winds of the moment. Successful churches follow a plan of where they want to go. This book will help you understand where you can turn for help, and how the Holy Spirit takes part in the process.

If you are involved in the life of a church, you probably know someone who has served on a Pastor Search Committee and/or you may have friends or contacts who have served in this capacity in other congregations. You will want to consult with them and listen to their experiences. They will tell you of their joys and frustrations, sometimes in laughter, sometimes in tears, or near to it. You will hear them comment about how difficult their task was because there were so many diverse ideas and an endless stream of potential candidates and most of all, that no one on the committee had previous experience doing this kind of work.

It is not unusual for people to serve on a Pastor Search Committee only once in their lifetimes. This means most everyone on a committee is likely to be a beginner. Most congregations need a new Pastor Search Committee only once every decade or so. In churches where the current pastor has served for 20 years or more, there was no call for a Pastor Search Committee in all that time. Sometimes an entire generation of church officers may pass without being called upon to search for a new minister.

Years ago, a friend called and asked if I knew anything about Pastor Search Committees. His wife had been elected to serve on one at their church. He wanted to know what he should expect as the spouse of a committee member. I told him, "There will be lots of lonely evenings for you, and trips out of town for her, and a great big sigh of relief at the end of the process." I also told him it would be a wonderful spiritual experience for his wife, and it could have benefits for him as well. Looking intently into what kind of a minister or ministry a Congregation needs or wants provides tremendous insight into the workings of the Church of Christ. It shows how many dedicated pastors and spouses are in active service to God, and how there are some of the other kind too. It forces us to reexamine our own call to service. Whether it is God's call to minister in a church or at the local plant or a department store or in our own communities, each and every Christian needs to be vigilant in seeking God's purpose for our lives.

Whether you are on the sidelines watching a Pastor Search Committee do its work or are a member of such a committee, you can be part of the process. I have found that if the whole congregation has input, and prays for the committee and the future of the church, the prospects for a successful journey to find a new pastor is immeasurably enhanced. Trying to discern God's call for your church will help you discern your own spiritual journey. Asking yourself what kind of a church you want your own congregation to be focuses your thoughts and prayers on the purposes of God for your life.

• • • • •

Hearing God's call to serve on the committee

In the Old Testament, God called Abraham, Sarai, Deborah, David, Isaiah, Jeremiah and a hundred more. In the New Testament, Mary, Peter, Lydia, Paul and the disciples of Jesus were all "called" to serve. The Lord continues to call individuals today. Hearing and responding to the call of God for service is a significant event for it reminds us of the ways leaders were called in the Bible. It encourages us to listen to what God might be saying to us.

In Genesis 12, God called Abram and Sarai from their

home in Ur of the Chaldees to go to a new dwelling place in "a land flowing with milk and honey." Six hundred years later, God called Moses while he was tending his father-in-law's sheep out in the wilderness near Horeb (Exodus 3). God sent him down to Egypt to lead His people back to the land He had promised to Abram. God asked him not only to lead the march up to the Promised Land, but also to lead their worship services and to be their prophet, telling them, "Thus says the Lord." He was to be their warrior leader, but also their pastor and counselor. Whenever they got in trouble, he would speak to the Lord on their behalf. At one point, the people decided to go back to Egypt, even though God had led them out to freedom through the Red Sea. Moses became so exasperated that he asked God, "What shall I do with this people? They are almost ready to stone me." (Exodus 17:4)

Throughout the Old and New Testaments, God continued to call individuals to do specific things. He called Deborah to be a judge, David to be a king, Lydia to lead a house church in her home town, Peter, Andrew, James and John to be disciples, Paul to be a missionary in the emerging Christian Church. In each case, God's call was clear, and He gave the individual an opportunity to respond. Sometimes they argued with God about their qualifications and the timing of the call. In the end they all heard and accepted the challenge. It is my hope and prayer that you are listening and have heard the Call of God to step forward to serve in selecting a new pastor for your congregation.

Today, God continues to call men and women to lead His church in a variety of settings and ways. In the pages of this book, we will discuss how that call is discerned through the workings of the Pastor Search Committee and, more importantly, through the presence of the Holy Spirit. You will find yourself using the situations and the stories in this book as metaphors for how to live out your own calling as well.

One large church in Texas decided to use a business model for calling their next minister. The Sunday after their founding pastor retired, five corporate jets left Houston early in the morning destined for cities where they believed the best preachers in America were about to preach their Sunday sermons. Each team planned to hear one of the preachers and then report back to the self-appointed committee on Monday night. Their goal was to have a preacher hired and ready to move to Houston by the end of the month. Others have hired expensive search firms to go and select new pastors for them, usually without success. The Church is different. God chooses to make it so and to guide the people of God in the most important selection a congregation will make in a lifetime of Sundays.

Many wish that a pastoral search could happen by gazing into a crystal ball, then flying off into the wild blue yonder and bringing us back the perfect minister. That model sometimes works in the business world when head-hunters set out to find the right person, but the methodology does not work in the church.

• • • • •

How can you prepare

This book will help you understand how a Pastoral Search Committee works, the ways the Holy Spirit is involved in the search and how each measured step and turn in the road is important to the search as a whole. As a book on travel recommends routes to take, places to stay and sights to see, so this book for a Pastor Search Committee will suggest what may happen in the journey. I will describe plans to make, meetings to attend, notes to write, travel plans to schedule, and ways to deal with the unusual tasks that lie ahead. If you are a casual observer of a search, it will help you understand what is happening when people who serve on the committee disappear several Sundays in a row or have to relinquish regularly scheduled activities.

If you are serving on a Pastor Search Committee, you will find yourself doing a multitude of new and different tasks. If your church's pastor served more than 10 years, you will need to conduct a study to help delineate your church's mission or vision. Many times the Church authorities and committees will require that some kind of Mission Study be completed before the search begins; especially if there have been difficulties. Times and circumstances change, and churches often discover their demographics have changed: for example, it is no longer comprised of young families, or its children have become young adults. Maybe the neighborhood has changed, and immigrant groups do not understand your church's language. Maybe a senior village has been built down the street, providing many potential members. All those issues and countless more should be considered by the congregation prior to looking for a new leader. It is valuable to take the time to discover, discuss and rediscover your church's history, faith journey and ministry.

If you have an Interim Pastor who is providing good leadership for the congregation he/she might also have skills to help with the mission study and the whole process of discernment. With the Interim in place the selection process can obviously proceed at a more leisurely pace. Sometimes the Mission Study is undertaken by another group before the Pastor Search Committee is formed. Some churches do not do a formal Mission Study at all. Whatever, the leaders of the congregation should be asking themselves and canvassing the entire membership about what kind of ministry God is calling them to, and more especially, what kind of minister can best provide that leadership.

Out of the mission study, the committee can write a short paper on the life and ministry of your church. This paper, known in the Presbyterian Denomination (PCUSA) as a Church Information Form (CIF), will provide good information to introduce your congregation to potential candidates and help you find a good match. If your church belongs to a denomination, the paper may be posted on the vocation or ministry page at "denomination headquarters." Pastors and new candidates for ministry learn about churches through this process. Committee members will read many resumes and Pastor Information Forms (PIF), which are biographies of the pastors detailing their education, interests and experience. Through prayer, careful reading and open discussions with other committee members, a list of potential candidates will emerge.

Once the initial prospective list of candidates is selected, each of them can be invited to submit audio tapes which committee members will listen to. Video tapes where available can be watched at committee meetings or by individuals. They will also spend hours on the phone checking and re-checking references and eventually participating in face-to-face interviews. Members of the congregation can help by praying for the work of the committee and suggesting candidates to the committee. They can encourage the Pastor Search Committee to take the time necessary to find the right person. Trust that God will lead the committee and your church to the candidate He intends to serve your church.

CHAPTER 1

RESPONSIBILITIES OF A PASTOR SEARCH COMMITTEE

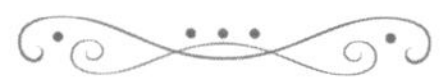

When you agree to serve on a Pastor Search Committee, you may or may not know exactly what the committee's responsibilities are. You can be sure, however, that other people will know or pretend to know exactly what the committee should do; and they will be more than willing to share their views with you. They will tell you that you are responsible for finding the best minister possible. You are to spare no expense. You are to climb every mountain, look in every glen, peer into the hearts of everyone who is and is not available and find the ideal minister for your wonderful church. Below is a description of the candidate for whom they think you should be searching:

The perfect candidate will be young (30 to 35), but have 25 years of experience. He (she) will be a masterful preacher who never uses a note in the pulpit, and who has been preaching for at least two decades. The person will be able to talk to the oldest members of the congregation as if they are old friends, but also be able to put youth and children at ease. The person will be able to make eight calls a day on older members of the congregation and have time to lead the youth fellowship group the same evening. The person will have a warm, wonderful touch with people, and be an administrative whiz.

He (she) will not only have ideas for every committee meeting, but will also attend every meeting and still be a strong family person who is home with his (her) children every evening.

Get the picture? Some members of your congregation will have firm ideas about the right kind of minister for your church. Listen to them but do not get sidetracked. You were put on the committee for a reason, hopefully having to do with your good sense and your ability to figure out God's will for your church.

Take your responsibilities seriously

The members of your Pastor Search Committee should do three things in the early stage of working together:

1. Get to know each other. This can be a relaxing time when you show the playful side of your personality. You may need some humor later on when you struggle over more serious issues.

At the start of each meeting, you may want to pose a question to each committee member; for example, name your favorite sports star, vacation spot, movie or song. And, of course, ask each other what each one believes and how they came to know the Lord and how they became committed to the Church. Knowing little details about each other will give you a deeper understanding of and appreciation for each other. This will be crucial as you work toward a common goal.

2. Get to know your church inside and out, because how you describe it to yourself will help to shape the perception of who the appropriate candidates will be to become your next pastor. You might begin the process by seeking out the best procedure for learning more about your congregation. Many ask if they should hold a series of congregational forums, or survey the congregation, or have a series of conversations with people who know the church well. As you work through these issues, keep in mind that the larger the congregation, the harder it will be for one committee or one person to know all aspects of the church.

It is also necessary to determine the extent to which your committee represents the church as a whole. Do you represent the church as it is today or as it will be in a few years? If your congregation is happy with the current worship situation, this will be transmitted to candidates. If the committee feels that worship needs to change dramatically, or that the current staffing is all wrong, this will be represented to candidates. It is not necessarily unhealthy for a committee to think ahead, but it could be a disaster for a new pastor if the Pastor Search Committee thinks the congregation has already settled on changes when it has not.

3. You are charged with finding not only the one you think might be the best person to be your new minister, but also the person God is calling for your congregation. This is an awesome responsibility. The good news is that you are not doing this alone. You not only have the help of others on the committee, but you also have the support of your congregation and the denomination with which you are affiliated. More than anything else, you have the full support of God in this task. Time and time again I have witnessed the powerful call of God working in mysterious ways through the life of a Pastor Search Committee.

• • • • •

Write a short purpose statement

To keep you focused, you should write a short statement of purpose. It will be a foundation that you can return to when you get lost and wonder what you are doing, It should be brief—no more than a short paragraph—and should be agreed on by all members of the committee. Here are four examples of purpose statements:

"We will call the person that God reveals to us through the best possible search using modern technology."

"The members of the Search Committee dedicate ourselves to being fully committed to reading, praying, and discerning the one to whom God is leading us."

"Using time and space to the best of our abilities, we will pray for and listen to the will of God working through us to find the person best suited to be the pastor of this church."

"We will seek to discover the purposes of God for our congregation and pray to be God's instruments as we strive to call the right person, male or female, young or old, interesting or challenging, to be our pastor."

In the search process, you will find it is easy to wander off the task. Remember: if you don't know where you are going, any road will get you there. Knowing your responsibilities will give you a good leg up on your work.

CHAPTER 2

LEARNING TO WORK TOGETHER AS A COMMITTEE

Whether you were elected, appointed, selected or volunteered for the Pastor Search Committee, you are probably delighted to serve in this very important position in the life of your church. It may not have dawned on you until your first or second meeting that the most immediate task will be getting along with other members of the committee. How well you fulfill your mission of calling the best pastor for your church is directly related to how well you work together.

Different members of your committee will bring different perspectives to the task. Some will see their service as a calling from God. Others will view it as a job that needs to get done. Some already "know" what kind of minister they want. You won't always agree with each other about the strengths and weaknesses of your former pastor or the qualities needed in a new pastor. This can actually create a healthy climate for discussion.

Just as pastors are called by God to a certain church, so members of a Pastor Search Committee may be called to this work. In his book, ***Listening to Your Life***, pastor and author Frederick Buechner said the following about a calling:

Like "duty," "law," "religion," the word "vocation" has a dull ring to it, but in terms of what it means, it is not

> *dull at all. Vocare (means) to call, of course, and a person's vocation is a person's calling. It is the work that we are called to in this world, the thing that we are summoned to spend our life doing. We speak of a person choosing their vocation, but perhaps it is at least as accurate to speak of a vocation's choosing the person, of a call being given and a person hearing it, or not hearing it. And maybe that is the place to start: the business of listening and hearing. A person's life is full of all sorts of voices calling them in all sorts of directions. Some of them are voices from inside and some of them are voices from outside. The more alive and alert we are, the more clamorous our lives are. Which do we listen to? What kind of voice do we listen for? (page, 159)*

Some of the committee members may be people with whom you worship every Sunday, share a Church School class or carpool with your children. Some may be friends with whom you enjoy socializing outside of church functions. You may never have had a conversation with other members until the first committee meeting. But for the next several months, you will have to get along with everyone.

Getting ready: Three things to do

The first thing you will discover is that you may have different thoughts about your former pastor. Some of you may have viewed him (her) as a great communicator, while others may have thought the pastor only shared the facts with close friends. Some of you may have felt the pastor was cold and impersonal, while others thought he (she) had Jesus' touch. Some of you may have appreciated every word he (she) preached, while others found their minds drifting during sermons.

The second thing you are going to realize is that you don't agree on what you are looking for in the next pastor. Some committee members may want a pastor who is highly relational, a pastor who knows everyone by name by the second week, always smiles and only gives answers that people agree with. Some committee members may want a pastor who is good with small groups, or loves to teach and can take the lead on intellectual topics. A few others may only care that they won't be embarrassed by what the pastor says or does.

Beware of falling into the trap of matching the new pastor's strengths against the weaknesses of the former pastor. For example, if your former pastor was lax in making hospital calls, you may want to find someone with a great bedside manner. If your former pastor was a terrible administrator, it is not automatic that you should seek someone who loves administrative work. If your former pastor kept ideas to himself or herself, you do not need to look primarily for a great communicator. If you do, you will replace one set of weaknesses with another.

The third thing you are going to realize is there is often one person on the committee who feels it is his or her divine right to pick the next pastor. A few members will begin to defer to this person at the first committee meeting. If you don't agree with this member's assessment of candidates, you are likely to find yourself on the outside looking in. The person who fills this role may be identified as the logical choice to chair the committee, but also may have refused to serve there. This person will miss some meetings, but will make sure his (her) opinion is noted or insist the committee wait to make an important decision until he (she) can be present. This person will often ask no questions during the first part of an interview, but will ultimately pose "the big question." This person might even attempt to intimidate a candidate by inserting an opinion into a question. For example, he (she) might say, "I don't see in your form where you have managed a church budget. How do we know you can do that?" What this person fails to recognize is that if the candidate was not qualified, the committee would not have invited this person for an interview.

Differences of opinion are signs that people hold values and opinions about which they feel passionate. Most committee members will be willing to discuss and compromise once they understand that others have different opinions.

How differences of opinion affect the choice of candidates

Joe and Sarah are members of the same church, but think about their church very differently. They serve on the same Pastor Search Committee. Sarah lost her husband five years ago and doesn't like to drive at night. Joe is the father of three teenage children. He has agreed to bring Sarah to committee meetings.

Sarah attends the 11:00 a.m. worship service every Sunday and a Women's Circle meeting each month. Years ago she was the Sunday School Superintendent. Joe is the head usher at the 8:30 a.m. service, attends Men's Bible study and is a youth leader on Wednesday nights.

Sarah doesn't understand why all members can't worship together in one Sunday service, why finding Sunday school teachers is such a problem and why the last minister left after only four years.

Joe hasn't been to an 11:00 a.m. worship service in five years, wonders aloud why a pastor can't preach two different sermons on Sunday morning and knows exactly why the last pastor left after four years—which, in his opinion, was not soon enough.

Both will need to amend their thinking about who will be the best candidate for their church.

It is important for the members of the committee to have an honest appraisal of what each person expects in terms of the next minister. Hidden agendas must be left at the door in order for the committee to do serious work.

Tentative timeline for completion of the work

When a Pastor Search Committee is selected, the members need to know how long the process will take and what kind of a time commitment it will require.

There are many variables that can affect the time it takes to call a new pastor. The committee may connect with a candidate in the first reading of a Pastor Information Form and move quickly to interview and call this candidate. It is also possible that after a lengthy search, the leading candidate will decline the committee's offer, forcing them to start the process over.

A realistic timeline for moving smoothly through all stages of the process is given below:

a.) Getting to know each other, writing a Church Information Form and having the form approved (2-3 months)

b.) Add two months if the committee does a Mission Study (2 months)

c.) Receiving and reviewing dozens of Pastor Information Forms, moving toward a goal of 8-10 candidates (3 months)

d.) Interviewing the top 8-10 candidates by phone (2 months) e.) Bringing your top 4 (or fewer) candidates for face-to-face interviews (6-8 weeks)

f.) Assessing the interviews and deciding whether or not to issue a call to one of the candidates (1 week)

g.) Allowing the candidate to pray about God's call (1 week)

h.) Holding a congregational meeting or official board meeting to present your candidate for a vote (2 weeks). At this meeting, the Pastor Search Committee is generally dismissed.

i.) Anyway you add that up, it normally comes to something like a year or more before the job is done.

Practical organizational issues

Always open your Committee meetings with a prayer and a short devotional. Let each member who feels comfortable doing this take a turn at leading this time of worship. It will help inspire and focus your meetings, and you will discover magnificent ways that members phrase their conversations with God.

Your committee will need to determine in advance how a decision on the final candidate will be reached. If it is by vote, you need to decide whether it will be by unanimous decision or majority decision; if the latter, what constitutes a majority in your case. Perhaps the committee will work toward reaching a consensus instead of voting. Deciding this early on will eliminate problems later when people will have assumed the process would be done a particular way.

The larger the committee, the harder it will be to reach a unanimous decision. You may decide that a majority for your committee is 80 or 90 percent. In a committee of 10, for example, a majority would require an 8-to-2 or a 9-to-1 vote. With a committee of 15, it would require a 12-to-3 vote. But the essential thing is that the committee agree in advance how the decision will be made. Minutes of the meeting should state the agreement clearly.

The issue of how often the committee will meet is also important. Weekly meetings will probably meet the needs of the committee early on. That may be a hardship for some committee members, if they had not considered this possibility when they agreed to serve and expected the committee to meet on a monthly basis. However, the early stages of a search require time preparing a mission statement, getting to know other committee members, writing a Church Information Form and determining the skills you are looking for in a new pastor. All of this takes time, and weekly meetings help speed along the process. Once you have finished this ground work, which should take approximately 3 months, you may settle into a routine of meeting twice a month or as needed. Pick a night or afternoon that works for everyone and block off those dates for the next three months. Everyone will not be able to attend every meeting, but when you miss a meeting, you must learn to trust the process.

You must also elect a chairperson. A good chairperson should be someone who is visible in the congregation, comfortable speaking in front of a large group and has the ability to run a meeting where there are differences of opinion. A good chairperson does not allow a committee meeting to get bogged down by members who discuss an issue to death, but allows many opinions to be heard. It is a delicate balancing act. A perfect chairperson will allow the voice of the minority be heard, but make sure the will of the majority is followed and that the meetings continue to move forward.

A corresponding secretary also should be chosen. This person will keep up with the task of writing letters to the candidates (see Appendix A), so it should be someone with organizational skills, who enjoys paper work.

You may also want to ask someone to take minutes of each meeting. This person may be called the secretary, but is usually a different person than the corresponding secretary. Due to the confidentially of your work, formal minutes of your meetings will not be presented to an official board, but they will help you remember what you have done and what decisions have been made.

Keeping the congregation informed

You will also want to schedule regular updates for the congregation. These can be done through monthly or bi-monthly articles in your church newsletter or announcements during worship services or in the church bulletin. Although much of the work will be confidential, comments can be made about completing the Church Information Form and making it available for congregation members to read after it has been approved, asking for names to consider and asking the congregation to keep the Search Committee in their prayers. You may want to tell the congregation about the need for confidentiality and ask them not to ask committee members about specific candidates or who the committee is considering.

CHAPTER 3

PORTRAYING YOUR CHURCH ON PAPER

All Pastor Search Committees face the challenge of describing their church or faith community to potential candidates in 10 pages or less.

If your church belongs to a denomination that offers support in the search process, you will be given a detailed Church Information Form to fill out. Some of the questions will be statistical in nature. Others will require a prose response. If you do not have a denomination-wide support system, you may want to design your own form. Sample forms may be available on denominational web sites. You may also go to the web site of other churches that are seeking pastors and look at their Church Information Forms. Most churches seeking pastors have a link to the form on their web page.

Keep in mind that you have only one chance to make a first impression. For most pastors, your Church Information Form will be their first experience learning about your congregation. They will be eager to learn which facts you share about your church.

Most pastors seeking a new position will read many Church Information Forms, just as you will receive more than 100 Pastor Information Forms to read. The pastor who is actively seeking a new call will receive at least two dozen church forms and may read many additional forms online. The seeking pastor will read every Church Information Form with an eye on the reasons to be interested or not interested in this church.

Writing your Church Information Form

Pastors will rate you on how well you tell your story. Different styles are used and for a while it was the "in thing" to give an outline:

We believe in God.
We believe in Jesus.
We believe in the Holy Spirit.
We are a community of believers.
We believe people really like us.

Our church is good at:
Worship
Music
Christian Education
Youth

This approach does not tell your story. Facts can sound like this for example: "The church committee chair walked into the room for the special meeting on church missions. The motion was to spend an extra $20,000 from the designated church funds. The vote was 6—2 in favor. They closed the meeting with prayer."

You have all the information in those sentences but there

is nothing compelling to grab your attention. You could have used these words: "The church committee chair was apprehensive as she walked into the room. One of the committee members had called her earlier in the day and voiced strong opposition to the special meeting. An extra $20,000 was being requested to help fund a new start up program for those who had lost their jobs recently because of the economic crisis. When another member of the committee told how he had been helped two decades earlier by a similar program and she saw a tear in two member's eyes as he shared his story, she knew the motion would pass."

When churches use bullets instead of prose to describe their ministry, it may give the impression they don't know what to say. On the other hand, some churches are too creative in an attempt to stand out. An example of overdoing creativity would be one we saw recently: "As one enters the sanctuary door of our church, the eye is immediately drawn to the stained glass rose window above the pulpit area. The window reminds us of the love Christ has for our church and the love members have one for another."

Or, "The giant oak outside the church's main door is the focal point for our congregational life as well as the life of the community. Standing alongside our church the 'oak' has been the center of the community square for more than two centuries. General Washington took refreshments under the 'oak' before the battle of … and the 'oak' has been an integral part of this community. People remember having a church picnic under the 'oak' as little children and returning to this place for marriage and the baptism of their children."

While these may paint a pretty picture, they provide little information about the church. When you are writing the description of your congregation, ask yourself whether the narrative describes your church for potential pastors or if it is more of a history of the church.

Don't be afraid to be creative if you have creative writers on your committee. Creativity is okay. However, it is important not to lose the vision of what you are trying to accomplish, which is to describe your church to someone who has never experienced it. You want the reader to understand about the ministry and mission of your church. Tell them what is important and move on. Remember, you may eventually have to explain some parts of this information form to a candidate in a face-to-face interview.

Some things to remember

Here are some guidelines to direct your writing:

- Choose someone who listens well to other peoples' ideas to write the form. This will ensure the form incorporates everyone's ideas, but flows seamlessly because it has only one author.
- Make sure the facts are correct.
- Make sure there are no contradictions in the form.
- Do not exaggerate what your church is doing.
- Do not exaggerate your dreams for the future.
- Do not type the form in capital letters.
- When you are finished, run "spell check" on the form.
- Ask a good proofreader to review the form.
- Take the task seriously, but remember that the Lord is guiding your process.
- You might also want to ask a ministerial friend to look it over in confidence and express an honest opinion to you.

The fact that many pastors will read your Church Information Form does not guarantee your favorite candidate will be interested in your church. Just because you have an opening does not mean that a pastor looking for a new call will fall in love with your church. Some committees have the attitude they are going to find the best person, whether they are available or not, and convince them they should answer God's call to come to their church.

I know one church where the Pastor Search Committee was convinced a minister in a neighboring state was the right fit for their church. They did everything they could to convince him to come. They attended his church every Sunday for six weeks to hear him preach, and took him and his wife out for lunch every time. They brought him a video of their community and their church. They had community leaders outside their church call him to tell him what a wonderful community they had. They asked the governor of the state, who happened to be a member of their church, to call him. They told him how many country clubs he could join if only he would come to their church. He told them politely but repeatedly that he was not interested; he said their Church Information Form did not "sing" to him.

When they persisted, he finally ended the pursuit in a way they would never forget: He said, "I don't like your state, I don't like your town, I don't like your church. Are we clear here?"

While this may be an extreme example, it illustrates that sometimes you just can't get to first base with a candidate of your choosing. Keep in mind that you don't know what is going on in his (her) life. Don't be offended or take it personally. God is calling you to look elsewhere, so be open to where God is leading you.

How much detail should you include?

Providing particular details on the Church Information Form can be helpful to candidates. For example, you might say, "We are involved in 20 mission ministries in our community. These include helping a single mother and her two children adjust from an abusive situation, feeding 75 homeless people once a week and running a support group that does grocery shopping and letter writing for AIDS patients." You have signaled how involved you are in community outreach, mentioned three compelling projects and detailed a life-threatening situation that is important to your community in fewer than 50 words.

If the Church Information Form rambles, candidates will assume that your church is unfocused and disorganized. If you pick out one particular element of your church and emphasize it to the exclusion of everything else, they may think this is all you are interested in.

Don't lose sight of the fact that your Church Information Form is not a permanent document. It will not be published, and as soon as you have a new pastor, hardly anyone will refer to it again. See it for what it is. Use it wisely. Then move on to the next part of the search process.

How important are statistics?

Can someone draw a clear picture of your church from statistics? The answer is: yes and no. Some ministers know the ins and outs of a statistical analysis of a church. For example, a church should have twice as many baptisms as deaths in a year for it to be a thriving, growing congregation. New growth is determined primarily from "professions of faith" or "adult baptisms," rather than transfers from other churches of the same or similar denomination. Income from living donors is more important than total income for the year, because total income might include a one-time bequest, endowment income or funds from a rare capital fund drive.

Some pastors will be especially interested in the statistical information. Knowing what the numbers reveal about your church will help you answer their questions. For example, a candidate might ask why your church membership took a 25 percent drop two years ago, why worship attendance was higher 10 years ago than today or how you kept Church School attendance so high when you were without a pastor. You might want to get one of several books on what these numbers mean. Denomination Resource Centers will have up-to-date book lists to help identify one that fits your situation.

Knowing how the information is used will help prevent you from making false claims about your church. No one enjoys saying their church enrollment is declining, but if your statistics paint a picture of a church that is not experiencing growth, be honest. You may want to emphasize the potential for improvement that could be realized by a minister with energy for evangelism. Or, if the numbers suggest your budget is increasing, but that the increase is the result of a recent capital campaign or a bequest, you should share this information on your form.

One pastor who was considering five churches of similar size made the short list at all five churches and was scheduled for on-site visits. He made a chart of the statistical information from each church, including their membership, gains and losses, baptisms, church school attendance, worship attendance, pledging units, amount pledged, mission giving and total income. His chart included a five-year analysis for each church. This enabled him to see immediately the trends and potential problems, and allowed him to ask important questions at the interview. Today, many denominations provide a 10-year statistical analysis of each church on their denomination web site page.

Salary and compensation information

In many congregations, members of the Personnel, Human Resources, Finance or Budget committees, help the Pastor Search Committee develop an attractive compensation package. Basic information about salary range and compensation is posted on the Church Information Form.

Many forms do not include a maximum salary. However, if you are using a denomination computer matching process, the maximum salary figure will be used to match a pastor's cash salary requirement against your maximum offer. Low numbers for minimum and maximum can limit the number of computer matches, as well as the number of self-referrals you will receive.

The salary you provided your last pastor is a good place to begin. You may decrease the figure to adjust for circumstances such as a long tenure or increase it because you are seeking a pastor with more years of experience than your last pastor. Keep in mind that if your salary offer is too low, it may eliminate potential candidates who are seeking a certain salary figure.

If your congregation has a church owned house they are

offering the new pastor he or (she) may take advantage of a special benefit. Pastors who live in a manse or parsonage may have a housing allowance but it must be designated by the congregation for a certain amount of money each year and the money can only be used for maintaining the manse or parsonage. This would include housing expenses not paid for by the church, including utilities, furnishings, repairs and improvements the pastor wants to make. Pastors with these living arrangements should not include the fair rental value of the parsonage or manse as income for federal income taxes. The amount the church designates as a housing allowance is not reported as wages on the pastor's Form W-2 at the end of the year. However, if the allowance exceeds the actual expenses, the difference must be reported as income by the pastor. This is a very important tax benefit for pastors living in church-provided housing.

Some congregations offer clergy who live in church housing an allowance in lieu of equity that the pastor is not accruing. This is figured by the amount that the housing market has increased or decreased in your community over the last year. When there is a decrease, no equity allowance is given for that year. To estimate this, take the appraised value of the home (say, $150,000) and multiply it by the trend in the housing market—for example, a 2% increase. The pastor would receive an additional compensation of $3,000, which could be put in a separate account for the time the pastor leaves your church and possibly must purchase a home.

If a housing allowance is offered in lieu of church-owned housing, someone from your committee will need to speak with a realtor to learn if it will be possible to purchase a home the pastor would be happy with at a price your church can afford. This is a critical issue in some small communities where a limited number of homes are available. Be sure to set an annual housing allowance that will provide good housing for an average-sized family in your community through mortgage payments or rental. You may want to ask if your church would be willing to lend the new pastor money for a down payment.

Someone on the Pastor Search Committee should discuss all housing options with the appropriate church board that monitors these funds and knows the tax implications of such a loan for both the church and the new pastor.

In order to arrive at a total compensation package, the committee must also consider health benefits, pension, a disability rider, a death benefit that might consist of an insurance policy equal to the annual salary of the pastor, a business expense allowance, funds to cover continuing education activities and any other benefits the church provides for its pastor (see Appendix B).

Also remind the appropriate committee of the church to budget for the cost of moving the new pastor to your community. If the new pastor lives further than 500 miles away, the moving expenses can reach $10,000.

Listing the skill sets you want in a new pastor

You are now ready to identify the qualities you seek in a new pastor. You will want to list these skills—usually no more than 10—on the Church Information Form.

Selecting these skills can be a time-consuming process, but well worth the effort. From an initial list, you may decide that some skills are required and some only desired. Pastors are also asked what skills they consider to be their gifts, and what they would like to do in their new call. If you use a denomination vocation agency, your church's list and pastors' lists will be compared in the matching process. If you are selecting your pastor without the help of a denomination, you will have to match the skills yourself.

Your Mission Statement may be helpful in identifying the pastor skills your church wants and needs. In the Mission Statement, you identified areas of ministry that your church does best or that your church is identified with.

You may have difficulty interpreting what some terms on the Church Information Form mean. There are subtle, but important, distinctions between certain areas of responsibilities: for example, worship leadership and preaching. Do you check both areas and use two of your required skills in the same relative area of worship? Do you assume a good preacher would also be skilled in worship leadership, thereby using only one of your required areas? What about adult ministry and family ministry: are they the same thing? Is mission beyond the local church the same as cross-cultural collaboration? At this point in the process, you may wish to engage a denomination executive to help.

It may be valuable for each person on your committee to rank their individual preferences first. After this is done, score them with the whole committee, and then identify areas of agreement and disagreement. To do this, each person can assign a numerical value to the skills they consider "required." Add up the numerical numbers for each skill selected by the committee and average them. You probably will have consensus on two or three skills, with several others requiring discussion. The skills that are not considered "required" can top your list of "desired" skills. Do the calculation and discuss "desired" skills.

You can speed the process by asking each member to do this ahead of time and email the numbers to one committee member, who tabulates the results and brings them to a meeting for discussion.

This process will be time-consuming, but you will be rewarded later on when you read Pastor Information Forms. It will help you eliminate pastors whose skills lie primarily in other areas. If you are a mission church and a potential candidate says, "I don't think mission beyond the local church is important," or if you consider preaching to be a critical skill and the form says, "I think personal contact with people is where I shine, and not my preaching," you may want to move on.

CHAPTER 4

READING AND GRADING PASTOR INFORMATION FORMS

As I have mentioned you can expect to receive at least 100 Personal Information Forms and resumes during your search—somewhat fewer if you are searching for an associate or assistant pastor. The number you receive is directly related to the number of ministers in your denomination who are seeking a call. Today, about one-third of the ministers in many denominations are open to a new call, and some are serious about relocating. Others are just wondering what is available.

You may hear from graduating seminary students looking for a first call, or ministers currently practicing outside the church who would like to re-enter church work. They may be involved in college teaching, directing a community social service agency or working in industry.

If your denomination has a placement service, they will forward Pastor Information Forms to you. You may also receive others from your district minister, presbytery executive, or other person who handles personnel matters in your conference, district or presbytery. Still other forms will come from individuals whose resumes you have requested.

A growing number of candidates send their information by email. Some denominations provide email addresses for the conference, district, or presbytery contact person and the designated person on the Pastor Search Committee who downloads and distributes Pastor Information Forms. Some committees send letters to all churches of a certain size in their denomination asking if the head of staff or senior minister knows anyone who might be interested in your church's position. This practice can often lead to good referrals. Committees also ask seminary presidents and executives of their denomination for referrals.

In addition, your committee should consider advertising the position in a denominational or interdenominational magazine. The ***Christian Century, Christianity Today, Presbyterian Outlook*** (or other denominational periodicals) are good places to advertise.

You want as many people as possible to know that your church is looking for a new pastor. The upside is you will receive many names and Pastor Information forms. The downside is you will have to read all of them.

If your denomination has a referral system, you will probably receive 15 to 30 forms immediately after the matching process begins. These are the pastors that your denomination feels would be the best match with your church.

Please remember that Pastor Information Forms are highly confidential information. Do not let anyone outside the committee see any of the forms, and do not talk about the forms with people other than committee members.

What to do when the forms arrive

Your first job is to decide which candidates deserve your serious consideration. Your goal is to select eight to 10 candidates you would like to pursue. You may want to use a letter grade system such as A for ones you want to consider, B for those you don't want to discard and C for those you will eliminate immediately.

Or you can use a numbering system where 1 is the highest and 5 is the lowest. You definitely want to talk to the 1s and maybe the 2s; you don't want to discard the 3s and would reconsider them if the 1s and 2s don't work out; you are not interested in the 4s and 5s. This system enables you to tally the scores on each candidate from every committee member and divide the score by the number of committee members to achieve an average.

Each member of the Pastor Search Committee needs to be open to the work of the Holy Spirit in this process and understand that God will lead you to the right person if you allow God to. Pray for guidance before you start to read, and never read more than 15 pastor forms without taking a break. Then pray again.

Most pastor forms will be about 10 pages in length. If there is an approved form for your denomination, check to see whether the form has been used. If a candidate has not used the form, you might want to ask why. The form should include basic information concerning the candidate's education, background, work-history and ordination status. The person should also answer the questions on worship, pastoral care, theology, administrative abilities and interests outside the ministry.

Most denominations also include a simple declaration that no sexual misconduct charges have been filed against the candidate. If sexual misconduct charges were filed in the past, the form should also tell you how the issue was resolved and what the consequences were. They might include counseling, a time when his or her ordination was set-aside or a civil or church court procedure.

One person should be designated to receive the Pastor Information Forms by email or U.S. mail. This person should keep a log of every form received, the date it arrives, who sent the form and the final outcome (see Appendix C). The record will be helpful should duplicates arrive months apart, or when someone calls and asks where you are in the decision process regarding this candidate.

Pastor Information Forms should be distributed to the committee members by email as soon as they arrive. If a committee member does not have an email address, the form should be printed out or copied and delivered to the committee member in a timely manner. It is not wise to have a church secretary or volunteer be involved in this or any other part of the Pastor Form process. You should not tempt others to read confidential information by putting it in their hands.

A friend in Pennsylvania was thinking of making a pastoral change. He didn't want anyone in his church to know he was open to a new call, and so he asked everyone he contacted to keep it confidential. However, his Pastor Information Form went to a church where a secretary was asked to make copies. The secretary happened to have an aunt who lived in the minister's town and attended his church. She mentioned to her aunt that they had received a Pastor Information Form from her minister. Before the end of the week, everyone at my friend's church knew that he was being considered for another call. At the next session meeting, the leaders suggested he resign.

This is one reason why you must treat the information as

confidential. Forms for persons no longer under consideration should be immediately shredded or destroyed.

What to look for

Make sure the candidate has answered all the questions, used proper grammar and spelled all words correctly. If the form does not meet your standards, the person may not measure up in other ways. Misspelled words or bad grammar may indicate poor attention to detail. Much of ministry involves written material, and it is important to know how to write.

When I was starting to write my doctoral dissertation, my faculty advisor told me a major publisher had recently asked him to review a book. He was appalled to find three grammatical errors in the first 60 pages. He returned the book to the editors with a note saying, "If you can't do a better job of editing a book, don't waste my time." While most of us would not have such high standards, we do have to have standards, and the appearance of the Pastor Information Form is a first good clue to the diligence and character of the person who wrote it.

The content is also important. Always check the dates of college and seminary graduation to make sure they make sense. If the person took time off between college and seminary, does the form indicate what he (she) did during this time, or are there unexplained gaps in the work history? If so, circle those dates and ask the candidate what he (she) was doing during this time.

The candidate should use language you can understand. If you cannot follow the logic of the information on the form, you may not be able to follow the logic in a sermon. If the language used is geared for a seminary audience, the candidate may have difficulty communicating with the members of your congregation.

Someone on the committee might find "red flags" in a pastor information form. Maybe the person moved three times in the last five years, or attended a theological seminary that is not accredited. In which case it is likely that candidate can be set aside in the initial separation. If the candidate seems otherwise worthy, you might ask for a clarification on the issues which present difficulties to the committee.

It is critical to know whether the candidate's theology matches the theology you are looking for. If you are an evangelical church that believes Jesus is the only way to salvation, and a candidate writes that God may include non-Christians in heaven, you may not want to consider this person any further. If your candidate writes that teaching the Bible is a great interest or loves to meet people in small groups to talk about faith issues and your congregation is looking for those qualities you may have a potential match. Or, if you have a wonderful community mission program that includes ministry to anyone who comes, and the pastor writes that passing out religious tracts on Saturday morning down on the street corner is his (her) idea of mission, you probably don't want to consider this person.

When you read a Pastor Information Form, the candidate's passions should be clear, and you should understand what he (she) really likes to do. The pastor's skills and desires should match those listed on your Church Information Form. You should get a gut feeling about a match during the first read. If you are not good at sensing this yourself, someone else on your committee may be excellent at it. Listen to the person who has this gift.

Reducing the list

The evaluation process is designed to help you reduce the list of candidates to the eight to 10 persons you are interested in pursuing.

Designate a meeting to discuss pastor forms. Make sure everyone knows which forms will be reviewed at the meeting.

Each person gets one vote on each pastor form. At the meeting, the first order of business is to give everyone a chance to share their grades and opinions. The grades will then be tallied to gain an understanding of where the committee as a whole stands on the candidate.

If one committee member is consistently out-of-step with how the committee is grading the candidates, you might want to ask how that person is doing their evaluation. Maybe he (she) misunderstood the process or, perhaps, honestly has different opinions. If this is the case, it would be a good time to stop and revisit what you are looking for in your next pastor. Review your Purpose Statement and the list of desired skills you highlighted in your Church Information Form. Pray together that God will guide you through this process. You may conclude that this committee member will always have a contrary opinion, and if so, accept it for what it is and move on.

Be aware that some ministers are very good at writing Pastor Information Forms. They may be better at writing forms than doing actual ministry. You may be excited to meet this person and hear him (her) speak, yet you could be terribly disappointed. Some candidates present themselves well on paper, but do not communicate well in other ways.

• • • • •

Inform candidates you have rejected

Once you have consensus on the candidates you are no longer considering, notify them immediately. Assign someone to write them a courteous letter telling them they are no longer being actively considered for the position (see sample letter in Appendix A). A letter enables you to put your best foot forward and helps ensure your congregation will be remembered well.

It is important to let all candidates know where they stand with your committee. Once you have narrowed your list to eight to 10 names, it would be wise to assign a committee member to be the contact for each candidate. This person will be responsible for corresponding with the candidate by mail, E-mail or phone. The candidates should be told that if they have any questions, they should call their assigned person on the committee.

There may be a number of candidates that you do not wish to release immediately, even though they are not on your short list. Hang on to these people for two reasons. First, you might find that some of your favorite candidates have already taken another call. Second, you may lose candidates further along in the process if the phone interviews don't go as well as expected. When this happens, you might want to reconsider candidates on the B list instead of starting over. However, at some point you must either include or release these candidates. As a matter of courtesy do not forget about them. When you are pleased with your final candidates, or when you are ready to call someone to the position, go back and notify these people that they are being released to seek a church elsewhere.

Sending a letter will also prevent you from reconsidering

someone who was initially rejected. It may seem hard to believe you would ever do that, but committees can come under tremendous pressure. Months after you have read someone's form, you may get a phone call from a church member whose relative was rejected. "Can't you please reconsider this person because he (she) is going through a real crisis and needs a ministry change?" they may say. Or maybe an influential denominational official will ask you to do a personal favor of considering someone you have already rejected. If you can say, "I appreciate your interest, but we have already informed the person that he (she) is no longer under consideration." Believe me, you will save yourself some trouble.

When you begin to receive pastor forms you will need a system to keep track of everyone. One way to do that is with a Log Book. (See Appendix C for more information) It is a good idea to note how you received the Pastor Information Form. Indicate whether it was a self-referral, came from denomination headquarters, was requested following the suggestion from a church leader or arrived from another source. When you send a letter of rejection, include a note mentioning how the form was received. It makes a negative impact to send a letter saying, "Thank you for sending us your form" when the person has been referred. Appropriate wording is not only considerate, but will help build good relations for your church down the road.

CHAPTER 5

MAKING A SHORT LIST OF CANDIDATES

You should reduce the number of candidates to eight to 10 for several reasons. First, as explained before, it gives you some flexibility. You may lose a couple candidates to other churches or because they are not interested in your church or community. Remember that most candidates seeking calls are dealing with multiple churches. Some may be further along in the call process than you are.

Second, a list of eight to 10 enables you to get acquainted with your serious candidates. The next stage will be to get more information from several sources by checking the candidates' references and conducting telephone interviews. You may also decide to visit the candidate's place of ministry.

Third, whittling your list down to eight to 10 stops you from being impressed with how many people are interested in your church. Sure, it is flattering to receive Pastor Information Forms from 100 ministers, but it is time to get on with the process. Believe with all your heart that God is leading you to one person on your list of names.

Why bother to check references?

You can check a candidate's references at any point in the process, but be sure to do it. Ideally, the task should be assigned to the person on your committee who is the candidate's contact. This will allow the person to form an impression of the candidate that can be transmitted to the committee.

Because references provide positive information, some people may wonder about the value of bothering with this step. It can be an effective way of obtaining new information indirectly. One time I called one reference, who proceeded to tell me what a great person the candidate was, how well he managed his church life, how well he was liked by people in the community and how hard he worked. Then he said, "I just don't understand why he has had such a hard time with his marriages." I knew the candidate was divorced and soon to be married for what he told me would be the second time. Through this conversation, I learned this would be marriage number three.

The references will tell the candidate that they have been contacted. Therefore, checking references is a signal to a candidate that you are interested in them for the position.

You may want to ask your candidate for additional references who are not listed on the form: for example, someone who supervised the candidate in another job, or local officials or businesspeople in the town where the candidate lives. If you decide to do what are called secondary reference checks, you should clear this in advance with the candidate. If you have close friends or family in the candidate's town whose confidentiality you can trust, it could be good to seek an additional channel of information.

Sample questions to ask a reference

You may wish to consider asking the following questions when talking with references. I recommend that you be consistent with each one:

- How long, and in what capacity, have you known the candidate?
- Is the candidate a self-starter? Can you give an example?
- Does the candidate need to report to someone, or can he (she) work alone?
- What are the candidate's more impressive characteristics?
- What areas of improvement does the candidate need to make?
- Can you describe a situation in which you witnessed first-hand the candidate's involvement in ministry? What did he (she) do? What were the results?
- Would you like the candidate to be a pastor for your family?
- Would you hire the candidate to work for you?

Phone interviews

The second thing you will want to do is set up a phone interview with the candidate. You may use a speaker phone or arrange a conference call on a speaker phone or through a teleconferencing dial-in telephone service. Be sure to let the candidate know which method you are using.

There are many variables that can affect a phone interview. The telephone connection may not be good enough that everyone can hear and understand the candidate. To the candidate, the committee may sound like it is sitting in a well. Furthermore, lack of face-to-face communication can make the interview awkward.

Sometimes, it can be difficult to discern if the candidate has heard a question. Other times, you may wish the candidate had stopped answering a question five minutes ago.

The process can be facilitated by dividing the committee into teams of three or four members to conduct telephone interviews. Fewer people asking questions should allow more time for answers. It will also be easier to find a speaker phone that works for three or four people than for seven to 10.

It is best to have a game plan for the phone interview. Be prepared with a short list of good questions (see Appendix D). If you want the process to last no more than 60 minutes, decide in advance how to manage that time. It might be broken into the following segments, which should be given to the candidate in advance:

- Committee members introduce themselves to the candidate (5 minutes)
- Candidate provides background information to the committee (5 minutes)
- Each committee member asks 2-3 questions (30 minutes)
- Candidate asks questions (15 minutes)
- Wrap-up and goodbyes (5 minutes)

The person on the committee who is in charge of the phone interview should manage the interview process. Do not allow one person to ask more than one question at a time.

The committee will get better at phone interviews with practice. I suggest doing a couple practice phone interviews with family members or friends. It is valuable to learn what it sounds like to be on the other end.

After the interview has ended, do a short evaluation of your impressions. Were you surprised by anything the candidate said? Did the candidate seem genuine? Did the candidate sound interested in your position? Jot down your thoughts as well as the team's consensus.

A committee that works hard can conduct 10 phone interviews in a two-week period. This enables all candidates on the short list to be evaluated in a short time frame, unless a candidate is out of town or unavailable during that period of time.

After the interviews are over, the hardest work begins. If you thought that reducing the list from 100 names to 10 was difficult, now you must cut the list of eight or 10 in half. By this time, the candidates are beginning to take on shape, form and personality. Everyone on the committee will have more opinions about them. But you can't bring 10 candidates to town for face-to-face interviews, so you must now use your best judgment and prayerful consideration to pare the list down to four or five candidates.

Most likely you will have gathered enough information to easily eliminate one or two. Maybe another one will take himself (herself) out of the process.

Visiting a candidate

A third way of getting to know your candidates is to visit them in their home church. This is the best situation for the candidates, who will be more comfortable in familiar surroundings.

If you want to visit a pastor, you must decide how many members of your committee will make the trip. The visit should be planned with the candidate so it can be done in a reasonably confidential manner.

It may be difficult to find a confidential place for a group of committee members to meet with the candidate. Since pastors are often public figures, many are known in their communities. If the candidate lives in a small town, people may ask why their pastor was talking with three strangers last week at a local restaurant or showed up to meet people at a local motel.

If you attend the pastor's service on Sunday morning to hear him (her) preach, be discreet. Do not sit together or sign the Friendship Pad using full addresses, particularly if the church is not located in a tourist town. One committee visited me, sat together in the same pew and signed in with complete addresses. When the Evangelism Chair reviewed the pew pads on Monday morning, this fact jumped out. He came into my office and wanted to know why I thought four people with different last names from the same city had attended our worship service.

Visiting a candidate in his (her) home church will allow you to observe how he (she) leads worship in a familiar setting, which should tell you how he (she) would lead worship in your setting. It will give you good information to bring back to the committee. For economic reasons, many committees rely on audiotapes and videotapes, but I encourage you to visit if it is practical, affordable and works for your church.

You have now acquired a substantial amount of information about your top candidates. You have conducted phone interviews, checked references and perhaps visited the candidates in their home church setting. This would be a good time to provide your candidates with more information about your church. If they haven't requested bulletins and newsletters, offer to send them. Since many candidates learn about churches by visiting their web sites, you may want to make sure your church's web site is up-to-date and accurate.

Audio and videotapes

The optimal way to evaluate a pastor's ability to lead worship is to witness it in the pastor's current church setting. However, it is not always possible to visit every candidate's church.

The next best option is to request audiotapes or videotapes from your list of top candidates to determine who the best speakers are. Most committees now request several tapes from each candidate, unless their church broadcasts streaming video of their worship services. Churches of all sizes are trying this technology, so be sure to ask about it.

Listening to an audiotape is like listening to a radio broadcast. If your committee is on a limited budget, I would suggest you request audiotapes.

Requesting a videotape is a less effective way to evaluate a pastor, even though you will be able to see the candidate's facial expressions and witness the congregation's response. The downside is that most churches do not make good videotapes. You will have to watch a tape shot by an amateur videographer. Both the video and audio quality may be poor.

If you televise your services, request a video if one is available. If you are not looking for a television star, I suggest you visit the candidates you are really interested in, or ask for audio tapes. The task of a Pastor Search Committee is to find the best pastor for your church. You are looking for someone who will be dealing with people in your congregation, in your family, and with you personally. It is certainly cheaper to ask for a tape, but watching the person work in his (her) own environment may tell you more than whether the candidate can deliver a sermon you can follow.

Contacting your finalists

As you start to contact the candidates on your short list, you should begin to assemble a calendar for the next stage of your work. Keep in mind that there are certain dates when your candidates will not want to talk with you, schedule a meeting with you, visit your church or move to your community as your new pastor. Times when it is unwise to contact a pastor include:

- Mondays. Many ministers take Mondays off. For others, it is a day to recover the energy expended on Sunday. It is an intrusion to call a pastor on a Monday. If your candidate takes a different day off, find out which day it is and do not contact your candidate on this day.
- December. The month of December is an extremely busy time for everyone in a church. Do not bother your candidates in December. It is a good time for your committee to take the month off to reflect on the candidates.
- The first two weeks of Lent. Lent is a busy time when many churches start new programs.
- Palm Sunday to the Monday after Easter. Pastors work every day during this period and may also be busy writing their Easter sermon.

Likewise, after you have reached a final decision on a pastor and have called and elected him (her), keep in mind the following start dates would be difficult:

- Any time during the school year, if the pastor has school-age children. A summer move would be preferable. As a second choice, the start of the second school semester might be acceptable.

- December. Never ask a pastor to start a new call in December. If candidates are in a loving relationship with their former church, they will not want to announce they are leaving right before Christmas.
- Mid-Lent through Easter. Pastors do not want to move during the days leading up to Easter, because their plates are full.

The best time to start a new pastorate is August 1. It allows the pastor a few days or weeks to settle in and get acquainted with the community before the fall begins.

The second best time is February 1. The winter holidays are over and the Lent/Easter cycle has not yet begun. It is easy to muster enthusiasm at the church, as people are looking forward to spring and new beginnings.

The third best time is June 1. This gives the new pastor an entire summer to settle in and get acquainted. There may be time for a little vacation before serious work begins. The downside to June is that many people are gone and it is more difficult to generate enthusiasm for a new pastor among the congregation.

CHAPTER 6

PLANNING GOOD FACE-TO-FACE INTERVIEWS WITH YOUR CANDIDATES

When you are ready to invite a candidate to meet your committee, it is up to you to ensure the candidate, his (her) spouse and your committee members get the most from a weekend visit. To this end, nothing beats a good plan. The visit is expected to include:

- Informal time for the committee and candidate to get to know each other.
- A tour of the church property.
- Time to see the community.
- A formal interview
- Hearing the candidate preach in a neighboring church that is approximately the same size as yours. Local denomination leaders can generally arrange this with several weeks' notice.

How to make sure things will go badly

The following story is about an interview that went badly from the start. It is a classic representation of what not to do. Real people, who represented a very good church, wanted to put their best foot forward. However, they forgot important details, planned poorly and when things went wrong, appeared to be unaware.

The candidate was invited for an interview. The vice-chairman of the Pastor Search Committee confirmed the candidate's travel plans in advance, knew what flight he was taking and what city he was coming from.

But when the candidate arrived at the airport, no one was there to meet him. He waited for 30 minutes, thinking someone must have been delayed in traffic. He finally began wandering through the terminal. One hour after his arrival, he spotted two people with name tags who were obviously looking for someone. When he introduced himself to them, they said, "Thank God you are here. We forgot the flight number and the name of the city you were flying from." It was a true confession, and he gave them a few points for honesty. However, the visit was off to a rocky start.

The candidate followed the couple to the car. As he opened the front door, he saw the front seat was covered with dog hair. Without an apology, the man said, "I ran my Irish Setters this morning, and they left some hair on my front seat." Wearing his dark navy suit, the candidate sat down among the dog hairs.

The committee members then announced that the "major interview" would take place in 60 minutes, and because they had a 30-minute drive to the location, they would have to swing by a fast-food restaurant to grab a bite to eat.

They finally arrived at a private home for the interview. After rapid introductions to everyone on the committee, the first question seemed to come out of nowhere: "What makes you think you are qualified to be our pastor?" Still reeling from the events of the day, he thought for a moment and then said,

"You have read my dossier. You should have some idea as to why I would be qualified to serve as your pastor." The remaining questions were less hostile, but the first question put him on the defensive, and he kept wondering who was going to try to ambush him next.

By the next morning, he felt he should have said: "I'm not qualified. Take me to the airport." It would have saved a whole weekend and, perhaps, helped the committee focus on what it was doing poorly.

The interview continued for two hours, with the committee grilling the candidate, who was not given time to ask any questions. At the end of the interview, he was told he could ask questions tomorrow. Unfortunately, this interview was the only time when every member of the committee would be present.

When the interview finished, a member of the committee took the candidate to the church to tour the facilities. No one was present at the church, and the person showing him around did not have keys for all areas, including the church nursery. If you are interested in attracting young families, this is an important area of the church property.

Two committee members took the candidate to a local restaurant for dinner, and then drove him back to his hotel. Although they were located less than 10 miles from a major city, no attempt was made to show him the attributes of the community so that his family might know what to expect if they moved there.

On Sunday morning, the candidate preached in a neighboring church. The committee member who drove him to the church told him how much he hated this community. He said, "I don't know why you would be interested in moving here. It is just hell with traffic and congestion." This was not a good way to inspire a pastor for the morning's task. The church had an attendance of about 25 in a sanctuary that would seat 500. It would have been much easier to preach to these 25 people, plus the 8 committee members, in a sanctuary that held 100.

After a pleasant lunch, two members of the committee took the candidate back to the airport. He asked them what the next step would be. "Would you like me to write you a letter? Will the chairman call me or should I call him? " he asked. "We'll be in touch with you," they responded.

The candidate was put off by the entire experience. After one week, he had heard nothing from the committee. Having given them a reasonable amount of time to get back to him by mail or phone, he wrote them a letter saying he was no longer interested in their position. He was surprised when he received a response saying they were sorry.

Many things went wrong that weekend:

- The weekend was not well planned.
- Members were not well informed or did not remember the few things that they were told.
- Committee members were not in attendance for the whole weekend.
- The committee did not try to sell the community where the candidate might be living in the near future.
- The worship situation was difficult.
- The committee gave the impression they were not interested in any questions the candidate had about the position.
- The committee failed to get back with the candidate after the weekend in a timely manner.

The committee could have redeemed the weekend by:

- Telling the candidate they had forgotten the air flight number and asking what they could do for him (her).
- Asking what he would most like to do or see during the visit.
- Attempting to put everyone at ease with a little humor when a hostile question was asked in the interview.
- Responding to the candidate's question about an evaluation of the weekend or getting back to him sooner with a note of thanks.

When a visit goes badly, it is an important thing to acknowledge what happened, ask what you can do to make the experience better and learn from this experience so you do not repeat your mistakes. There is usually plenty of blame to go around, but it is never very helpful to play the blame game. You have entered the pastor search as a learning experience. It is time to humble your spirits as you let God lead you into this crucial stage of the process.

What to do right

To have a successful visit, try to find several successive weekends outside of Lent and Advent when you can bring the top candidates to your community. Don't schedule the visits months apart, yet don't schedule more than one candidate per weekend. A five-to-seven week period is ideal for bringing three or four candidates to your community.

A tight time frame for seeing all final candidates benefits

everyone involved. If the weekends are too far apart, the first candidate will wonder what is taking so long for you to make a decision. The committee will also forget how impressed or unimpressed they were with the first couple of candidates if too much time elapses between experiences.

Do the best you can to schedule them closely. If one candidate can't come during the time period, consider that the Holy Spirit may be telling you something. When I was in seminary, I had an interview on the campus with a church that was looking for an assistant pastor. The two people who came apparently liked what they heard, and I was invited to come to the church on a certain weekend in April.

Unfortunately, I had two final exams the Monday following that weekend, and so I said, "I'm sorry but that is a bad weekend for me because of my test schedule." They told me they would get back with me, but they never did. Years later I learned more about that church's leadership and determined they would not have been a good fit for me. I advise you to listen when the Holy Spirit is speaking to you.

Always be honest with candidates when they ask where they stand with your committee. If a candidate is one of 10, tell them, and let them know what your schedule is for whittling down the number of finalists. If he (she) is the second interviewee, and two more are scheduled over the next three weekends, tell them that as well.

It is also fair to ask the candidate if he (she) is considering other churches and where he (she) is in the process. Some may be reluctant to share that information, but it never hurts to ask. This will help both you and the candidate understand the urgency in making a decision.

Be discreet!

Although honesty is the best policy, it is not wise to tell a candidate that he (she) is your favorite candidate. It sets the course for bad things to happen.

A committee chair once told a friend of mine that he was his favorite candidate. The chair went on to say that the committee would be making a decision the following week, and that my friend could expect to get a positive phone call. But things didn't work as expected.

Word had leaked out that the pastor was considering another call. When the phone call came, the chair said, "I'm sorry. You know you were my choice. However, the committee went with someone else."

By then, his church had heard that he was seeking a position elsewhere and asked him to resign. He was able to relocate six months later, but the whole affair could have ended badly.

Making a schedule for the visit

Make a schedule for each candidate's visit and give every committee member a job, such as picking up the candidate at the airport, touring the church, touring the community, making dining arrangements, driving the candidate to his (her) Sunday preaching engagement and returning the candidate to the airport to fly home.

A weekend visit should keep everyone busy at important times, but also allow the candidate some time to reflect on how things are going. One committee chairman took me to his mountain cabin on Saturday afternoon to relax before the big committee interview. It was very thoughtful and it gave me more energy for the interview and the remainder of the weekend.

A typical weekend might go as follows:

> ***Friday afternoon***
>
> Candidate (and spouse) arrive. Light social event includes dinner with committee and, possibly, their spouses.
>
> ***Saturday morning***
>
> Tour of the church and community, followed by lunch.
>
> ***Saturday afternoon***
>
> Interview with the committee.
>
> ***Saturday evening***
>
> Early dinner, allowing the candidate to return to the hotel early to prepare for tomorrow's sermon.
>
> ***Sunday morning***
>
> Preaching engagement at a neighboring church. Ask when the candidate is expected at the preaching location, and also ask the candidate how far in advance he wishes to arrive at the church. Be sure you have the details of the candidate's flight home, and if you will be driving the candidate from the church to the airport, be sure to pack his (her) luggage. The same agenda applies should the candidate chose to drive to meet you.

The committee should:

- Make the schedule.
- Review it together to be sure it makes sense.
- Familiarize everyone with the schedule.
- Email the schedule to the candidate and follow up to make sure it was received.

Assigning tasks to committee members

Make a chart of duties with the following categories:

- Sending a gift basket to the hotel before the candidate arrives. The welcome gift should include something from the church and something representing the community.
- Touring the church
- Touring the community
- Arranging for food and lodging
- Finding and preparing the room where the interview will take place
- Driving the candidate to his (her) preaching engagement
- Returning the candidate back to the airport

There are plenty of tasks to go around. Remember you will do this four or five times in the next five to seven weeks, so you can assign one committee member to the same duty for every candidate, or you can rotate assignments.

Please note that the person handling food and hotel accommodations should know how your church plans to pay the bill. Make arrangements before the candidate arrives to use a church credit card or to reimburse the committee member for using his (her) own personal credit card. Late one Friday night 15 years ago, I was checking into a hotel when the clerk asked for a credit card to cover the room payment. The committee member accompanying me never uttered a word. I finally produced a credit card. The church reimbursed me later for the hotel expense, but I still remember this as a bad experience. It was a detail the committee should have handled before the hotel clerk asked the question.

If you are wondering whether to pick up the candidate at the airport or let them rent a car, here's a story to consider: One church thought they were doing me a favor by not picking me up at the airport. They reasoned this would give my wife and me an opportunity to rent a car and familiarize ourselves with the area on our own time. Although that was a reasonable thought, they didn't take into consideration that we had arisen at 3:30 a.m. to make a 6:00 a.m. flight that landed at 11:00 a.m. in another time zone. They had also forgotten how difficult it is to find your way from the airport to a town 80 miles away. They never dreamed there would be an accident in front of the car rental place that would delay us an hour. We finally found a place for lunch at 2:00 p.m., and were still one hour from the church. Informal interviews with the church staff were scheduled to start at 3:30 p.m. We finally arrived at the church at 4:30 p.m. after encountering road construction delays, which at least one committee member seemed to know about. "You should never have come that way," he told us. While it didn't destroy the weekend, it didn't get it off to the best start. Go the extra mile and pick up your candidates at the airport.

The most important aspects of the visit

For the committee, the two most important aspects of the weekend are the interview and the candidate's preaching opportunity. The candidate will also consider these important, but will also value touring the church facility and hearing the vision the committee has for their church. Enough time needs to be given to these important items.

The candidate may also want to know the church's impact

in the community and its attitude toward change.

It is important for the candidate and his (her) spouse to see the worship space in order to visualize himself (herself) in that setting. Sharing a videotape of a service with the candidate could be invaluable. The candidate may also ask to be allowed to attend worship service, a church school class or other activity anonymously. If a candidate makes this request, be sure to honor it: there is no better way to get to know a church.

CHAPTER 7

CONDUCTING "THE BIG INTERVIEW"

Your committee's interview with the candidate will be the single most important activity of the weekend. It will give you an opportunity to observe how the candidate handles himself (herself) under pressure and responds to questions on a variety of subjects.

Develop your questions ahead of time

This is your interview, so you should be well-prepared. Your committee should spend time reviewing potential questions to ask the candidates (see Appendix E). For example, your committee might decide on questions in the areas of Christian education, pastoral care and worship. Or they might want to ask questions about the candidate's ability to manage people or work with volunteers. Questions should be specific. Asking, "Have you ever worked with volunteers?" is not a good question, because the answer, of course, is yes. A better question might be, "What style do you use when working with volunteers? Do you pitch in, recruit and watch or teach and lead by example?"

The committee chair or his (her) appointee] should be in

charge of the meeting. Each committee member should be prepared to ask at least one question. Topics should be decided in advance. For example, one person might handle Christian education, another ask about stewardship, etc., so all major areas of church life are covered. Be sure the first question is one that allows the candidate to share a personal story. Asking the candidate about his (her) faith journey or relationship with Jesus Christ would be a good starter. Save technical questions such as, "What do you think of our worship service times?" or "What do you think of our CE program?" for later.

When you ask questions that pertain to candidates' past on-the-job performance, don't be reluctant to request additional information about what they did or said in particular situations or the results of their actions. After all, you will need this data to discover their track record in dealing with important issues or areas of ministry.

The interview schedule

Decide ahead of time what you want to accomplish during the interview. The schedule might look something like this:

- Provide food and drink before the interview begins. This will help make everyone comfortable before serious work begins.
- Opening prayer by someone other than the candidate
- Introductions of committee members (15 minutes)
- Candidate talks of self and service, their faith journey or how they experience Jesus in their life (10 minutes)

- Questions from the committee (30-40 minutes)
- Questions from the candidate (20 minutes)
- Wrap-up, announcement of what's next on the schedule and closing prayer (5 minutes)
- Refreshments

The committee chair should be sure the interview does not last longer than 90 minutes unless, by common consent, everyone agrees a few more minutes are needed to finish up. The committee chair should bring the meeting to a close at the appropriate time and thank the candidate.

Candidates have questions and concerns, too!

The candidate should be allowed at least 20 minutes mid-way through or at the end of the interview to ask questions.

Your candidate will be concerned about the worship life of your congregation. It will be important for you to learn the style of worship your candidate feels most comfortable leading. If the pastor comes from a congregation with a praise service, for example, and your congregation favors traditional worship, you need to ask your candidate whether he (she) would want to start a praise service after arriving. If your church has a praise service, you will want to know if the candidate has experience in or a desire to lead such a service.

Related questions include the frequency and style of celebrating the sacraments, and the number of weekly or Sunday worship services. Candidates will want to know your perception of the openness of the congregation to change. Unfortunately the saying, "We are all for progress around here; it is just change we can't stand" is often true. Does your congregation take change in stride, or is every change a struggle regardless of how minor it is?

Candidates will want to know the theological climate of your congregation. Is there a mix of theological beliefs, or is the congregation more narrowly defined in a common belief system? Would your congregation identify itself as evangelical or progressive? Is it open to persons of diverse beliefs, or does it more narrowly define who "belongs" there? When I served a congregation that Anita Hill joined, one member said to me, "I didn't know that we were that inclusive."

If you make candidates feel at ease and find common ground where you can bond, their personalities will emerge and you can sense whether they are fun or serious, comfortable or anxious. Do not help them tell their story. Do not interrupt or coach them.

Assessing the candidate

As the interview moves along, ask yourself, "Do I like this person?" It is a simple question, but it's an important one, since ministry is about establishing relationships. If you leave the interview saying, "Wow, I really enjoyed that conversation," then you have learned something valuable. You want to determine whether the person is someone you can relate to and would like to know.

Also ask yourself if the candidate has the desired and required skills established in your church profile. Most candidates will do what they enjoy doing, no matter what your needs are, so make sure they will enjoy doing the ministry tasks that you have laid out.

Finally, ask yourself if the candidate fits your church. Ministers flourish in churches where they are not fighting the system, and members are better served when the minister and congregation share the same values and vision.

At some point during the interview (or privately during the weekend) someone from the committee who feels comfortable with the subject should ask about the candidate's financial requirements, should he (she) accept this call. The candidate should have an idea of the potential salary range from the material on your Church Information Form. You could start by asking about their current financial package. This is public information in most denominations, since most calls must be approved by the congregation. Follow up by asking what the candidate would expect in a new call. You need to take into consideration your community and the community where the candidate currently lives, the amount of responsibility in this call and how much your congregation can afford.

Pitfalls to avoid

I was involved in one interview that seemed to be disorganized. The members asked me a few questions about how I did this and that. About 40 minutes into the interview, the chair said to me, "Would you like to see the church manse?" So we all jumped up, got in cars and drove two miles to the manse. After about 30 minutes of looking around, we drove back to the church, got back in our chairs and continued the interview. After a few more minutes, the chair said to me, "Would you like to see the sanctuary?" So we got up from our chairs and went upstairs to see the sanctuary. After a short time, we went back downstairs and concluded the interview. I didn't get bored with the action, but it was not the best use of the time, and it did not help to keep the interview on track.

Another pitfall is allowing the candidate to take over the interview. You can sense this is happening when the pastor begins to ask questions or answer questions that no one is asking. For example, a committee member asks about sermon preparation, and the pastor takes the opportunity to talk about what a wonderful teacher and scholar he (she) is. Or maybe the candidate says early on, "Let me ask you a question." If it has nothing to do with the previous question, this is an attempt to move the interview to ground the candidate wants to cover.

The committee chair should steer the interview back on track by saying, "I don't think you heard the question that Jane was asking. Jane, would you restate the question, please?" Or by saying, "I appreciate your question, and let me assure you there will be time for you to ask this and other questions before we conclude this interview. Right now let's concentrate on Mel's question."

Take care to ensure there is time for the candidate to ask questions. The committee provides the candidate with valuable clues as to how a church functions. If you do not allow time for questions from your candidate, it gives the impression that you do not listen to the pastoral leadership of your church.

A chilling tale

Do not discount the role of the location where the interview can take place. Having a welcoming space for the interview is critical. Be sure the room has good ventilation, regardless of the season of the year, and that the furniture is comfortable. Arrange the setting so that everyone can see each other easily:

a circle or semi-circle is usually best.

My wife and I went to visit a church one fall weekend. The interview was scheduled to take place on Saturday morning at the church. That Friday night was the first cool evening of the year, but no one on the church staff had thought to turn on the heat before leaving on Friday afternoon.

When we arrived for the interview, it was about 60 degrees in the room. Sitting on metal furniture made it feel even colder. Moreover, the tables in the room should have been taken out of service 15 years earlier, or at least covered to prevent people from getting splinters. It was not a welcoming room.

When you set up an interview in a room at the church, ask yourself, "Does this room offer a warm setting for this meeting? Does it give a positive message about our church?" If you don't have a good room for this purpose, explore alternative options. It is perfectly acceptable to use a conference room at a hotel, bank or university building or a private home. If you use a home, make sure it is large enough to accommodate the number of people you expect, that other members of the household are otherwise occupied and quiet, and that the telephone is disconnected or someone other than the host is home to answer it.

Meeting with denominational leadership

If your church requires it, you may need to set aside some time during the weekend for the candidate to meet with denominational leaders. Churches that have a common form of government or a common constitution that binds the congregations together may require the appropriate denominational committee to review the candidate's fitness for your church.

In some cases, this meeting can be postponed until you have identified your final candidate.

Usually, the examination goes very well. However, the committee should be aware that if the candidate does not successfully pass the examination, in all likelihood you will be forced to remove the candidate from your list. Generally, the regional denomination officer will flag a problem candidate long before the person becomes a finalist for your position. On some occasions, however, this will be the first time the regional representatives meet your candidate.

If your candidate is rejected, it does not mean that you have done anything wrong. It simply means this candidate does not fit the requirements for membership in your denomination's local association. Most regional denominational bodies set their own rules for membership. These rules are usually compatible with those of the national or international denomination, but some have local applications that prevent some candidates from serving in a particular location. If you lose a candidate this way, just chalk it up to experience. Don't try to argue with the local or regional body: That is an argument you cannot win.

Processing the interview

After the interview is over, find time for the Pastor Search Committee to discuss the interview, when their impressions are fresh. This can be done by breaking into small groups immediately after the interview, and each group meeting with the committee chair. Don't delay the process: after a few days have passed, you will forget some key elements of the interview.

If meeting immediately does not work for your committee, consider filling out the Interview Score Card in Appendix E during the interview or shortly after the interview has concluded.

There should also be a discussion of the committee's general impressions of the candidates' intangible skills. Is this someone they would trust? Does the candidate have good interpersonal skills? Does he (she) seem credible and convey a sense of caring? Does he (she) have a sense of humor? You are looking for a well-rounded candidate who can handle a lot of different situations.

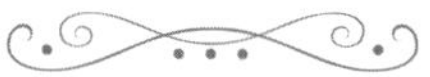

CHAPTER 8

CLOSING THE CALL

Hopefully you addressed the issue of how your committee will agree on a final candidate at the start of the search process. You need to know whether you require a unanimous decision, or merely a majority. If it's a majority, what percentage— how many votes—need to be "yes." The more people you have on your committee, the less likely a decision can be unanimous.

As I mentioned earlier, the committee might settle on a majority of 80 percent (six "yes" votes on a committee of seven, 12 "yes" votes on a committee of 15). Although it is wonderful when a committee reaches a unanimous decision, don't let one or two people prevent the remainder of the committee from making the decision they feel is right.

Another issue for the committee is, "What if we don't get our first choice?" You may not want to go to the congregation and tell them you were turned down by a candidate. It is immensely satisfying to get your first choice as your pastor. However, this is God's choice—not your choice. It might take the Almighty a couple of times before your committee gets this message.

One committee who interviewed me was manic about not being turned down. A member of the committee told me during the interview weekend that I was not being positive enough. Some members said they felt I was just going through the motions. I assured him this was not the case. Then one committee member said, "We want to know if you will accept this call if we offer it. We want to go to the congregation and tell them that no one turned us down, that our candidate was our number one choice."

I was put off by this attitude. I did not feel it was right to tell them I would take a call before the position was offered. I called them a few days later and told them I was no longer interested. However, I told God that if the committee came back to me after I told them no, I would take that as a sign that this call was from Him. They never called me, and the candidate they eventually chose stayed less than a year.

The process of finalizing your decision

You should allow for a two-hour meeting to decide which candidate you would like to call to be your pastor. Even if you sense that one candidate is the clear leader, allow time to process each candidate. Be doubly sure you open this meeting with prayer, and possibly allow each person to offer a sentence of prayer asking for discernment and blessings during the process.

Take about 10 minutes to review each candidate. The committee member who was the candidate's primary contact should present all relevant information about the candidate. Then the committee members should be invited to give their impressions. If you have three or four candidates, this could take 60 to 80 minutes. In discussing each candidate, you may hear a consensus emerge on one candidate. This would be a good time to use the Interview Question Score Card to remind everyone of how they evaluated the candidates in each of several categories. Also, refer to the required and desired skills for your pastor and recall how each candidate measured up.

After each candidate has been discussed, it is time to make a decision. You may want to take a break, giving your committee members a chance to get up and move around, get something to eat or drink and talk informally for a few minutes. Then either by consensus or by vote, the committee should formally decide on one candidate. At this point in the discussion, you probably know who your leading candidate is. The committee chair should suggest the name of the leading candidate and formally place that name in nomination as the next pastor. Then a verbal consensus should be taken, or a secret ballot from each committee member should be used to see how everyone feels about the candidate.

If there is opposition to the nominee, it would be wise to stop and ask the opposing member or members to talk about why they disagree. Ask if they would like to put forward another name from the list of candidates. If only one person is opposed, you may wish to ask, “Although you are not voting for this candidate, can you support him (her) as our next pastor?” Hopefully, you will stay in your committee meeting until everyone can agree on a positive response to that question. If there is a major disagreement on a candidate, it may be wise to adjourn the meeting and meet a week later, allowing time to settle the issues.

Asking the candidate to accept your call

Once you have decided on a candidate to be your pastor,

the next step is to ask the candidate if he (she) is willing to accept your call or your invitation to be presented to the congregation.

Part of your discussion will be the compensation package that your church is willing to offer. You may have had conversations about compensation during the interviews, but they were only preliminary discussions. Now you have to present a compensation package to the congregation or to the governing board that approves personnel matters. Many pastors will want to hear about the compensation package before they give you an answer. This is expected: people in any line of work generally want to know what a position pays before they agree to accept that position.

You can lose your candidate if the negotiations are not done correctly. If the pastor feels the committee is not treating him (her) fairly, the candidate could decline to accept this call. The person doing the negotiating for the church should be a member of the Pastor Search Committee. If you want to bring in someone else who knows more about the church's finances, make sure the candidate knows the committee member has the final say.

What your previous pastor made is a good starting point for discussion, which needs to be frank and to the point. The candidate should lay out his (her) financial needs, and the person doing the negotiating needs to know how flexible the church may be in this matter. Although the candidate will have seen the minimum and maximum salary figures posted on your Church Information Form, most people think in terms of a minimum 15% salary increase when they change jobs. Having this conversation with the final candidate during the interview process before you reach this point will help set the boundaries for your conversation and allow for fewer surprises.

Pastor's compensation packages are generally public information. When a congregation approves the terms of call or the compensation package, everyone who attends the congregational meeting gets a copy of the terms. In denominations where a board approves personnel matters, three to 30 people may know what the pastor's compensation package entails.

In some congregations, the information causes controversy. Some people may think the new pastor should make substantially less than the former pastor, because he (she) is new to this position. Some people will compare their own salaries with the pastor's offer and conclude that the pastor is either overpaid or underpaid. You may need to tell the congregation why you are offering the new pastor more than you paid the former pastor. To those who think the candidate is making too much or too little, there really is not much you can say.

The second problem is that hard-nosed business people will want to know if the church got the best deal possible. What they mean is, "Did we hammer down the compensation package as low as we could get it? Did you negotiate well on behalf of our church?" You may respond by saying, "We think we are offering a fair compensation package that meets the candidate's needs and our church's financial situation." A new minister is not an item to be bought and sold. He/she is a servant of the Lord and deserves the best that we can give.

Negotiating a compensation package

Church members can be blunt when discussing finances. There is no need to try to intimidate your candidate. If you have an honest disagreement over compensation, try to work it out. Find out in advance what pastors of similar-sized churches in your area make. It might show you that you are right on target. Much information is available from your denominational headquarters and on other web sites.

Before you approach your final candidate, you should review the pastor compensation package as shown on your Church Information Form. Start with your previous pastor's compensation package as a point of reference. You might ask whether the candidate brings skills the previous pastor did not have, has experience at a church of the same size, lived in a community with a similar cost of living and will accept what you offer.

All income categories and benefits should be listed in the compensation package (see Appendix B). Those categories might include, but are not limited to:

- Salary
- Housing
- Deferred compensation
- Medical plan
- Retirement plan
- Continuing education allowance
- Travel and business expenses
- Book allowance
- Reimbursement for medical deductible
- Social Security reimbursement
- Vacation time
- Study leave time

In the best situation, both parties are happy with the outcome of the negotiation process.

The candidate you choose may be ready to respond immediately, or may need time to talk with family, friends or other people important to the pastor. The candidate may want to carefully consider all of the aspects of this call and to listen to the word of the Lord. If the candidate asks for time, it is important for you to allow it. One or two weeks would be reasonable.

If the candidate declines your call, it is normal to feel disappointed. However, it is usually not a good idea to ask the candidate to reconsider: you don't want someone who has serious questions about starting a new ministry. Take it for what it is. The Lord is leading you to someone else or leading this person to another ministry. It may be helpful to take a deep breath and ask what is God intending for your church. You may want to move on to the next candidate on your list of finalists. However, it will be necessary to evaluate why that candidate was not your first choice. You may also reconsider the candidates you have not discarded or start over with new Pastor Information Forms.

Starting date, official notifications and spreading the news!

You also will want to agree on a start date. Many congregations want a new pastor to start immediately, but the new pastor will need time to give notice at his (her) church and say goodbye to the congregation. The start date must also fit into the church calendar. The best times for a new pastor to start are, in order of preference, August 1, February 1 and June 1. If that timing does not work, make do with whatever works with your candidate. Please be mindful of the pastor's family situation. If the pastor has children in school, he (she) may have difficulty relocating in the middle of a school year.

When a candidate accepts your call to be your pastor, you will need to notify the other members of the Pastor Search Committee that your calling process is coming to a close. Then you will want to notify the leaders of the congregation, including the official board. They must begin to plan the next steps in the process. The interim pastor will need to know so he (she) can plan his (her) exit from your church. If you are a connectional church, you will need to notify the local district supervisor, regional pastor, presbytery executive, denominational committee or anyone else who needs to know that you are ready to call your new pastor.

At this point, you will want to contact the other candidates and inform them of your decision. Please be gracious about the process and thank them for allowing you to consider them for this position. Most candidates will thank you for your consideration and for taking the time to be in touch with them. Candidates could be called on the phone by the members of your committee who were their designated contact during the search process.

The Pastor Search Committee will need to have at least one more meeting to make arrangements to present your candidate to the congregation, to clean up any unfinished business with other candidates and to destroy all Personal Information Forms you have accumulated.

Presenting the candidate to the congregation

In most denominations, the congregation must vote on the candidate to finish the call process. The committee may want to mail a brochure to the congregation announcing their choice to the congregation. It should include a photo of the candidate and his (her) family (if applicable), a short biographical sketch page on the candidate's educational background and past ministry experience, and quotes from members of the committee as to why they support the candidate and quotes from a few of the candidate's references explaining why the person is a good choice for this congregation.

The committee may also want to plan an informal fellowship time prior to the congregational meeting for members of the congregation to meet the candidate.

If the candidate will be present on the Sunday morning the congregational meeting is held, the informal fellowship time can be done the day before. It should be a "cookie and tea" kind of gathering, with plenty of time for the candidate to chat informally with members of the congregation. This is not a good time to ask the candidate to make a 10-minute speech or to give his or her impression about the church. This situation is tense enough for the candidate, who must meet scores of new people. If the candidate's family members are present, a member of the committee should make sure they are comfortable and have everything they need.

Whether or not the candidate is present at the congregational meeting depends on the rules and traditions of your particular church. Some congregations want to experience the candidate leading a worship service and preaching a sermon before they vote. It seems better to most observers that it is fairer to the Candidate and the Congregation to have a chance to experience each other in worship. Other congregations, however, trust the committee to find the best possible candidate. You will need to check ahead of time with your denomination to learn what is required or recommended. And it might be wise, in either case, to canvass some members of the church to see how it was handled there with previous changes of pastors.

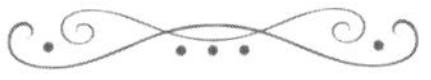

CHAPTER 9

ENDING THE JOURNEY

Most congregational meetings for calling pastors are held on a Sunday morning following the worship service. This enables the largest number of members to be present to help make this important decision.

The chair of the Pastor Search Committee should make the report to the congregation. If the chair cannot be present, the reason should be explained to the congregation. In such a case, the person who shepherded the candidate through the committee process would be the next choice for presenting the candidate to the congregation.

The presenter should make a thorough report to the congregation, beginning with a motion nominating the candidate as the next pastor. According to ***Robert's Rules of Order***, this allows for discussion to follow.

The presentation should explain the process the committee went through to arrive at this candidate, and should include:

- A review of how the Pastor Search Committee was selected, since new members may have joined the church since the process began.
- The committee's Statement of Purpose and how it led the committee through the process.

- How many candidates the committee brought to town to interview.
- Why this candidate was selected, highlighting the candidate's background and abilities.

Allow questions from the floor after the presentation. Generally, no questions are asked. However, the committee should be prepared to answer any questions that might be raised. Under no circumstances should the committee answer questions about other candidates.

The congregation should then proceed to vote on the motion. Individual church rules or denomination rules may specify how the vote should be taken, but in most congregations, it is done by secret ballot.

At this point most votes will be in favor of the candidate. Don't be surprised, however, if there are one to 10 votes against the candidate. Some members may feel that votes should not be unanimous. Most congregations have at least one contrarian who votes against almost everything. Someone may hold a grudge against a member of the committee, or someone may misunderstand the ballot.

If there is a significant negative vote, the candidate under consideration would be wise to prayerfully reconsider the call. While the term "a significant negative vote" is a vague term, it is often used in the jargon of the church. For some congregations it may mean more than 15 percent of those voting; for other churches, it might mean 35 percent. If this occurs, the Pastor Search Committee should consult with their denominational spokesperson or committee or, in a congregational system of government, with the church board.

The candidate will have told the committee that he (she)

is willing to accept this position upon the recommendation and positive vote of the congregation. After the congregation votes, the candidate needs to give a final "yes!" This can take place after the candidate is brought back into the room or by phone, if the candidate is not present for the vote. In some traditions, the question is posed to the candidate in front of the congregation, "Do you accept the call of God, as expressed by the vote of this congregation, to be our new pastor?" In other traditions, the formal question is part of the worship installation service for the pastor in the near future.

The last item of business at the congregational meeting is to dismiss the Pastor Search Committee. In most cases, this is a committee of the congregation, and because the congregation elects this committee, only the congregation can dismiss it. Have someone ready to make a motion to dismiss the committee with thanks. A specific termination date in the near future should be given in order to allow for any unfinished business to be wrapped up.

Transitioning the new pastor

The chair of the Pastor Search Committee may want to suggest that a transition committee be appointed to help the pastor-elect in the early stages of his (her) new ministry. Participants may include a member of the Pastor Search Committee and a member of the official board. They would be available to help communicate needs concerning:

- Housing
- Relations with the community and identification of community leaders
- Church office needs

- Church staff (If the pastor has ideas on using staff in different ways, the transition team could help communicate this to the official board)
- Church calendar (explaining the traditions of this congregation)

The transition committee could also introduce the pastor's family to the local school principal or potential teachers. They might help the family understand traffic patterns, where best to shop and how best to become integrated into the community.

Taking care of unfinished business

The work of the Pastor Search Committee needs to end by taking care of any unfinished business. This includes telling all candidates who have not been officially informed that you have called a pastor.

You should also make sure that all Pastor Information Forms are destroyed by shredding or other disposal. These forms are confidential, and must be treated as such. Any and all sermon DVDs, audiotapes and videotapes should be collected and erased or returned. They may be reused or recycled, but only after they have been erased and any labels removed.

The chair of the committee should also have a debriefing time with the official church board. The chair should be careful to disclose any special arrangements the committee has made with the pastor-elect, including:

- Reimbursement for a house-hunting trip prior to beginning work.

- The pastor's agreed-on start date.
- Vacation time the committee has negotiated for the remainder of the calendar year.
- A loan from the church to help with a down payment on a house.
- Other items the committee has arranged with the pastor-elect.

If you have church housing for the minister, be sure a representative in charge of church property inspects the house and makes any needed repairs. If you allow the new pastor and spouse to help make decisions about remodeling, painting, carpeting or other items that include colors and textures, be sure to forward this information to the pastor once the call is approved. Any repairs or remodeling will likely need to be done within a tight time frame before the new pastor arrives.

Saying a prayer of thanks

Your job is over. It has been an incredible journey. You can have a prayer of thanks together, knowing that God led your committee members to the right candidate.

For the last several months, you served on one of the most powerful committees in the church. People sought out your opinion. They questioned you about your secret meetings. They wondered about your travel schedule as you visited candidates.

Your participation on a Pastor Search Committee was a once-in-a-lifetime experience. It exists no longer: the committee was dissolved with thanks. One month after the new pastor is installed, you will realize that you are merely another member of the congregation. You have your life back. You can enjoy normal activities on Monday nights instead of rushing off to committee meetings.

If members of the Pastor Search Committee had disagreements, it would be a good time for some lighthearted relief. You might plan a fun evening together, with each member sharing one unforgettable moment at a committee meeting. It might be a way to mend any lingering wounds.

The committee might want to gather annually on the anniversary of the installation of the new pastor to party together with the pastor and spouse. When the committee is still pleased with their choice a year later, such a gathering can be a wonderful celebration.

The new pastor may seek out your advice from time to time, but he (she) will soon know other members of the congregation as well as or better than you. It is time for the special relationship with the pastor to be put in its proper place. May your prayer be that God richly blesses you and your new pastor, as this new phase in the life of your congregation begins.

APPENDIX A
SAMPLE LETTERS

1. Thank you for your information

Candidates whose names come from a matching process through your denomination or are referred from individuals may be unaware you have received their information. For those who have self-referred, a letter acknowledging receipt of their name or their Pastor Information Form is a courtesy.

Dear (candidate's name),

Your name has been referred to the Pastor Search Committee of the (name of your church) in (city, state).

We will review the information and get back to you soon regarding further consideration.

The committee is in the (beginning, mid) stage of our work, so it will probably be several months before we make a decision regarding our new pastor. Thank you for allowing us to consider your name. We will, of course, keep this in confidence.

We have enclosed information about our church. We wish you well in your ministry.

Sincerely

(your name)
Secretary, Pastor Search Committee

2. We received your name, but need more information

Dear (candidate's name),

The Pastor Search Committee for (the name of your church) in (city, state) has received your name for consideration for our position of Pastor. We need more information to consider you further. Would you please send us a current copy of your Pastor Information Form or a two-to-three page information sheet that describes your work, education and pastoral experience? If you do not wish to be considered for this position, you need do nothing.

We have enclosed information about our church. If you have further questions, please do not hesitate to contact me.

Looking forward to hearing from you, I remain,

Yours sincerely,

(your name)
For the Pastor Search Committee

3. You are no longer under consideration

Dear (candidate's name),

We appreciate your time and effort in sending information concerning your work in ministry. The Pastor Search Committee has carefully reviewed your information and feels that while your experience and qualifications are considerable, they are not a match for our needs here at (name of church) in (city, state). Your name is no longer under consideration by our committee.

We wish you the best in your ministry and in the calling God places before you.

Sincerely,

(your name)
For the Committee

4. You are still under consideration

Dear (candidate's name),

We recently reviewed your Pastor Information Form and are interested in pursuing our common interest. A member of our committee (if you know who it is, tell the candidate here) will be in touch with you soon about the next stage of our search. We are still several months from issuing a call to our next pastor, but we wanted to let you know of our progress.

The person who phones you will be your contact person throughout the search process. When you have questions, please feel free to talk with this person. He (she) will know where our committee is in the search process, and will be able to answer questions concerning our church and community. You can be assured there will be a friendly voice on the other end of the phone.

Sincerely,
(your name)
For the Committee

5. Confirming an onsite visit at the candidate's current place of ministry

Dear (candidate's name),

It was grand visiting with you on the phone last night. Thank you for your helpful information about your community. Members of the committee who will be visiting this weekend include (names). We have made reservations at the hotel that you suggested (name the hotel) and will plan on arriving on Saturday as we discussed.

You can be assured we will be as discreet as possible, not only during the worship service on Sunday but in meeting with you in public.

The schedule we worked out is enclosed. If you have any questions, please do not hesitate to call. Again, we look forward to being with you next weekend (include the dates).

Yours in Christ's service,

(your name)
For the Committee

6. Letter following a visit to the candidate's place of ministry

Dear (candidate's name),

Thank you for allowing our committee to visit you in your church and experience you leading worship in your current church. We felt at home worshiping with you and your congregation.

We enjoyed meeting you and your spouse (if applicable) and having some informal time to talk about your goals for the future and to share with you more detail about our ministry.

As the committee continues to evaluate the candidates under consideration, I will remain in touch with you. If you have any questions, please do not hesitate to call or send me an email.

Wishing you the best of the coming week,

I remain,

(your name)
For the committee

7. Arranging for the candidate to visit at your church

Dear (candidate's name),

The members of the Pastor Search Committee are excited about your impending visit. We have planned a weekend that will be informative about our church and community.

The enclosed schedule gives the specific times for activities and information about where you will be staying for the weekend. You will note there is some flexibility to allow you to add things or people you would like to see during the visit.

Your contact person (name inserted here) will be in touch with you prior to your arrival to go over the final arrangements concerning (flight information if arriving by air, rail information, or where the person is to go when arriving by car) and any other last-minute information.

Again we are excited about your visit and pray that all will go well in your life in the days ahead.

Sincerely,

(your name)
For the committee

8. Following up after the candidate has visited your church

Dear (candidate's name),

Thank you for visiting our church and community. Our committee enjoyed getting to know you (and spouse if applicable) in a more intimate way. We hope that your journey home was an enjoyable one.

As we mentioned during your visit, several other candidates will be visiting our church in the coming weeks. We would like you to remain under consideration for the position and will keep you informed of our progress with the search process. If you have any questions concerning your visit or your continuing consideration by the committee, please feel free to call or correspond with your contact person (name the person).

Wishing you the best in the days ahead, I remain,

Yours sincerely,

(your name)
For the committee

APPENDIX B
COMPENSATION PACKAGE TERMS

1. **Salary:** cash salary paid to the pastor.

2. **Housing:** money set aside for the housing needs of the pastor for rental or mortgage payments, utilities, and any other expenses that can be classified as housing expenses. This may include regular cleaning items for the home, and purchases such as a dishwasher, downspout or painting.

3. **Deferred Compensation:** Money excluded from income tax and FICA reporting that will be placed in an account and paid to the pastor upon retirement. Some pastors desire this as a secondary retirement plan.

4. **Medical Plan:** Medical plans that cover the pastor and his (her) family. It may be paid to a third-party provider, or into a denomination plan. Disability insurance may be included.

5. **Retirement Plan:** Money set aside for the retirement. Many denominations have a pre-set percentage payment, which is normally equal to 10-12 percent of salary and housing.

6. **Continuing Education Allowance:** Money used to

cover conferences, college courses, books, and other educational enrichment programs. The funds may be used to cover registration fees, cost of the study course, travel expenses, hotel and meals, books, etc. This is a reimbursement fund, and expenses are usually reimbursed after receipts and details of the expenses have been itemized. Sometimes, prior approval is required by the official board of the church or by the regional denominational leadership, before the expenses are considered reimbursable.

7. **Travel and Business Allowance:** Money used to reimburse the pastor for travel expenses (car depreciation or mileage), meals, or other expenses incurred in the performance of the duties of ministry. These should always be voucher expenses, with receipts obtained for all items. If the allowance is paid as a monthly stipend, it is fully taxable as income. If the allowance is based on voucher expenses, it is a business reimbursement and is not taxable.

8. **Book Allowance:** Money used to buy books and periodicals.

9. **Reimbursement for medical deductible:** Depending on the pastor's medical plan, there may be a large deductible before coverage begins. This reimbursement covers the deductible, or a portion of it. This is a voucher expense that requires receipts.

10. **Social Security Reimbursement:** Money that is used to pay the FICA quarterly payments. FICA considers pastors to be self-employed. The IRS considers pastors to be employees. This double classification causes unique problems. Pastors must file a quarterly statement and pay FICA 15.3 percent of their taxable income. Typically, the social security reimbursement covers the church's share, or 7.75 percent of the salary,

which is the rate the church pays for other full-time employees. Pastors must also either make quarterly payments for income tax, or have income tax deducted from their salary.

11. Vacation Time: This depends on church and denomination traditions. Many pastors get four weeks' vacation. Sometimes they trade a salary reduction for more vacation time. Ministry is a high-stress vocation, and vacation time is used to recharge batteries and relax with the family.

12. Study Leave: This depends on church and denominational traditions. Many pastors receive one or two weeks of study leave to attend conferences, catch up on reading, or take a college course in an area of interest or need. Some churches allow pastors to accumulate study leave over a three-year period and take six weeks in the third year for a directed study or for graduate work.

Some pastors negotiate a sabbatical after six years of service and place it in the call. This can be an incentive for the pastor to stay for at least six years. Sabbaticals are generally taken for three or four months after six or seven years of service. There generally is an agreement that the pastor will serve the church for at least one more year after taking a sabbatical.

APPENDIX C
CHART FOR KEEPING TRACK OF CANDIDATES

A well-maintained chart will remind you about the details of your contact with each candidate and save you from embarrassing moments when you try to set up a second phone interview with someone you talked with about six weeks ago.

Someone on your committee will love to keep up with such a chart. It is a positive way to note progress even when no progress is apparent.

<u>Candidate's Name   Current Position or Status</u>

Date of first contact . . . . ____________
How we heard about this candidate . . . . ____________
Grade given at the initial reading of pastor's form . . . . ____________
Phone contacts (every time we /she/he calls)
and by whom . . . . ____________
References checked (how many and by whom) . . . . . . ____________
Phone interview (small group) and when . . . . ____________
Phone interview (whole committee) and when . . . . . . ____________
Visit to the candidate's home church or
place of ministry. . . . . ____________
In town visit(s) (spontaneous or planned) . . . . ____________
Any special requests. . . . . ____________
Face-to-face interview date . . . . ____________
If, when and how the candidate's contact
with committee was terminated. . . . . ____________

APPENDIX D
ABOUT PHONE INTERVIEWS

1. Phone etiquette

a.) One person should be the phone contact for each candidate.

b.) Call the candidate and set up the interview.

c.) Make sure the committee can be present for the phone interview.

d.) Check out the speaker system ahead of time to

make sure it works.

e.) Conduct a sample interview so that you know what it sounds like on both ends of the phone.

f.) Send the candidate a detailed schedule for the interview, but do not send the questions you are going to ask.

g.) Make sure the candidate has time to ask questions.

h.) End the interview at the designated time.

2. Sample questions for the phone interview

a.) Tell us about your call to ministry.

b.) Why are you seeking a new call at this time? (Do not use this question with a seminary student or someone seeking a first call.)

c.) What do you consider your areas of strength in ministry?

d.) What are the areas in ministry that you have the most difficulty with?

e.) What book(s) have you read or what movies have you seen in the last year?

f.) Do you prefer to interact with people one-on-one, in small groups or in larger groups?

APPENDIX E
QUESTIONS TO ASK WHEN VISITING A CANDIDATE

a.) Tell us about your faith journey.

b.) Having read through our church information

form, what issues do you think our congregation needs to address?
c.) What would be your priorities during your first year as our pastor?
d.) Repeat some of the questions listed for the phone conversation so the whole committee can hear the candidate's responses.

APPENDIX F
INTERVIEW SCORE CARD

For use in face-to-face interviews with candidates
(Idea for this Score Card is adapted from Youth Ministry Architects, Nashville, TN, non-published.)

Circle the number that appropriately ranks the candidate's ability in each category.

Leadership/Strategic Thinking
Low 1 2 3 4 5 High

1. Describe a time when you encouraged others to share new ideas.
2. Describe your style and approach when leading a small and a large group, such as a Bible study and a Session meeting.
3. How do you keep yourself organized?
4. What was one of your best experiences as a minister? Describe the context and issues of the situation, what you said and did, and why this was a good experience.

5. What was one of your worst experiences as a minister? Describe the context and issues of the situation, what you said and did, and why this was one of your worst experiences.
6. How would you welcome strangers into a church service or group meeting?

Program Knowledge/ Passion for Ministry

Low 1 2 3 4 5 High

1. What criteria would you use to evaluate the current programs at our church?
2. In what areas of ministry are you now spending the most time? How do you like this arrangement?
3. What do you see yourself doing in five years?
4. Why do you want to be a minister or continue in your calling?

Management Style

Low 1 2 3 4 5 High

1. Describe a time when you processed a new idea under a particularly difficult circumstance. What were the issues and the context? What did you do? What were the results?
2. How would you describe your management style? Illustrate how you employed that style in a particular situation.
3. If we called a church where you have worked, what might a member or fellow staff member say

about you?
4. How comfortable are you in front of young people? Older people?

Problem-Solving

Low 1 2 3 4 5 High

1. Tell us about a conflict you have had in ministry and how you resolved it.
2. Tell us about a mistake you made in ministry.
3. Describe an experience where you worked with a staff member or volunteer who performed poorly. How did you help them bridge the gap?

Personality focus

Low 1 2 3 4 5 High

1. What do you do for fun?
2. What would you rather do—teach in front of a large group or a small one?
3. What is on the front of your refrigerator?

Spiritual

Low 1 2 3 4 5 High

1. Tell us what kind of role God plays in your personal life.
2. Tell us about your prayer life.
3. What does it mean for you to be a Christian?
4. What would you expect from a church where you serve?

5. What role does the Bible play in your spiritual life?

Denomination focused

Low 1 2 3 4 5 High

1. Why are you a Presbyterian (Baptist, Lutheran, or whatever)?
2. Have you ever considered leaving this denomination? If so, why?
3. From your perspective, is this denomination thriving or declining?

You may have other categories or questions, and that's fine. The idea is for each committee member to have a form they fill out mentally during the interview and physically after the interview. As an alternative, the committee can fill out one form for each candidate during the post-interview review. These are two ways of keeping track of the candidates in each face-to-face interview.

About the Author
Dr. W. Glenn Doak

Walter Glenn Doak was born in Eighty Four, PA. in 1946. He attended Sterling College in Kansas and he holds both the Master's and Doctor of Divinity degrees from Pittsburgh Theological Seminary.

He began his ministerial work as Associate Pastor at Southminster Presbyterian Church in Mt. Lebanon, PA. Then he was called to be Head of Staff at First Presbyterian Church of Norman Oklahoma in 1980. In 1996 he moved east to the First Presbyterian in Athens, GA, where he had to shift his loyalties from the Oklahoma Sooners to the Bulldogs of Georgia. Both Congregations have been quite successful under his leadership.

Glenn has served the Presbyterian Church at large in his active work in the Presbytery and Synod. He was Moderator of Indian Nations Presbytery in Oklahoma in 1993. He is currently active in Northeast Georgia Presbytery. His community service includes service on the Boards of the United Way, Human Rights Commission, Samaritan Counseling Center, Student Center Board President and Chairman of Presbyterian Homes of Georgia.

Glenn has been Director of the Church Conference for Large Church Pastors in Orlando, FL since 2003. He is also a valued Board Member of Desert Ministries Inc.

Glenn is married to Virginia Fulk Doak. They have three children –Melissa Schafstall, Ryan and Nathan Doak, plus three grandchildren, Owen, Evan and John.

DESERT MINISTRIES INC.
Current Publications Available

SOMETIME BEFORE THE DAWN: Responses to the Resurrection
Dr. Richard M. Cromie

YOU NOW HAVE CUSTODY OF YOU:
Christian Reflections on Marriage and Divorce - Dr. Richard M. Cromie

WHEN YOU LOSE SOMEONE YOU LOVE
Dr. Richard M. Cromie

WHEN A CHILD DIES - Dr. Daniel T. Hans

WHO REALLY LISTENS WHEN I SPEAK? - Jodie Huizenga

CHRIST WILL SEE YOU THROUGH - Dr. Richard M. Cromie

THE BEST IS YET TO BE - Dr. John Calvin Reid

PRAYERS AGAINST DEPRESSION - Dr. Lance Martin

RELECTIONS ON SUICIDE - Dr. Perry H. Biddle, Jr.

WHEN YOUR LIFE INCLUDES A WHEELCHAIR
by Marilyn Murray Willison

A TIME TO MOURN AND A TIME TO DANCE
by Evie McCandless

WHEN ALZHEIMER'S DISEASE STRIKES
by Dr. Stephen Sapp

A JOURNEY THROUGH CANCER
Dr. Melanie Bone and Dr. Richard M. Cromie

DYING WITH GRACE AND HOPE - Dr. S.Allen Foster

RHAPSODY OF SCRIPTURE - Dr. Richard M. Cromie

MY COMMITMENT - Dr. John Calvin Reid

HOW TO HELP AN ALCOHOLIC - Martin

HUMOR AND HEALING - Dr. Perry H. Biddle, Jr.

Please visit our web site: www. Desmin.org